The CBT
Art Workbook for
Coping with Anxiety

Part of the CBT Art Workbooks for Mental and Emotional Wellbeing series

The CBT Art Workbooks for Mental and Emotional Wellbeing series provides creative CBT information and worksheets for adults to manage and understand a variety of emotional issues. Suitable for adults in individual or group therapeutic work, they are an excellent resource to use in conjunction with professional therapy or for adults to use themselves to improve and maintain mental wellbeing.

By the same author

The Art Activity Book for Psychotherapeutic Work
100 Illustrated CBT and Psychodynamic Handouts for Creative Therapeutic Work
Jennifer Guest
ISBN 978 1 78592 301 2
eISBN 978 1 78450 607 0

The Art Activity Book for Relational Work
100 illustrated therapeutic worksheets to use with individuals, couples and families
Jennifer Guest
ISBN 978 1 78592 160 5
eISBN 978 1 78450 428 1

The CBT Art Activity Book
100 illustrated handouts for creative therapeutic work
Jennifer Guest
ISBN 978 1 84905 665 6
eISBN 978 1 78450 168 6

of related interest

Anxiety is Really Strange
Steve Haines
Illustrated by Sophie Standing
ISBN 978 1 84819 389 5 (Paperback)
ISBN 978 1 84819 407 6
eISBN 978 0 85701 345 3

The CBT Art Workbook for Coping with Anxiety

Part of the CBT Art Workbooks for Mental and Emotional Wellbeing *series*

Jennifer Guest

Jessica Kingsley *Publishers*
London and Philadelphia

First published in 2019
by Jessica Kingsley Publishers
73 Collier Street
London N1 9BE, UK
and
400 Market Street, Suite 400
Philadelphia, PA 19106, USA

www.jkp.com

Library of Congress Cataloging in Publication Data
Names: Guest, Jennifer, author.
Title: The CBT art workbook for coping with anxiety / Jennifer Guest.
Description: London ; Philadelphia : Jessica Kingsley Publishers, 2019. |
Includes bibliographical references.
Identifiers: LCCN 2018047872 | ISBN 9781787750128
Subjects: LCSH: Anxiety--Alternative treatment--Handbooks, manuals, etc. |
Cognitive therapy--Handbooks, manuals, etc. | Self-care, Health.
Classification: LCC RC531 .G84 2019 | DDC 616.89/1425--dc23 LC
record available at https://lccn.loc.gov/2018047872

British Library Cataloguing in Publication Data
A CIP catalogue record for this book is available from the British Library

ISBN 978 1 78775 012 8
eISBN 978 1 78775 013 5

Printed and bound by CPI Group (UK) Ltd, Croydon, CR0 4YY

Acknowledgements

I would like to express many thanks to all my clients and colleagues, who, over the years have helped bring this workbook into being. Grateful appreciation goes to the theorists who have devoted their lives and careers to helping people experience happier, healthier, and more peaceful lives. I've given credit to theorists where I've knowingly designed a worksheet from their work, and there are some pages designed from techniques I've come across over the years which I'm unfortunately unable to give specific credit to. No worksheets have been created without acknowledging the source where this is known. Thanks also to everyone involved at Jessica Kingsley Publishers for your support and input.

Contents

About This Book 9

Introduction 11

1. What Is Anxiety? 16

2. What Is CBT? 24

3. Observations 36

4. Cognitions 60

5. Emotions 89

6. Physiology 103

7. Behaviours 112

8. Different Types of Anxiety 117

9. Relaxation 152

10. Taking Control 165

References 171

About This Book

This workbook offers an opportunity for those experiencing anxiety to help manage and cope with the symptoms using tools from Cognitive Behavioural Therapy approaches. I've worked with many clients experiencing anxiety over the years and have found CBT approaches incredibly successful in helping to reduce symptoms, as well as for learning ways to help manage them. High levels of anxiety are something I've experienced personally during stressful times in my life, and this has given me insight and understanding of how distressing anxiety can be. It's a privilege to be able to share these ideas with you here, and I sincerely hope this workbook has a positive impact on your life and your emotional and mental wellbeing.

You are not alone

In 2016, Mind published the findings of a report (McManus *et al.* 2016) showing how many people in England were experiencing different types of anxiety. Figures are per 100 people of the population:

General anxiety disorder 5.9

Phobias 2.4

Obsessive Compulsive Disorder 1.3

Panic disorder 0.6

Mixed anxiety and depression 7.8.

Using this book

You might choose to focus on the pages most relevant to you, or work through the entire book from beginning to end. There are some generic exercises and others specific to a particular type of anxiety.

This book can be used autonomously or in conjunction with therapy. It's not intended to be a replacement for Cognitive Behavioural Therapy. Please ensure that access to professional support is available if you experience any unexpected or overwhelming emotional reactions as a result of working through this book.

The ideas here are based on CBT principles and yet the language I've used is slightly different from some traditional descriptions. The rationale for this is that I have observed how so many people who suffer with anxiety feel as though something is wrong with them and how some descriptive phrases can add to this sense. I've therefore described habitual patterns of thinking and behaviours as helpful or unhelpful, realistic or catastrophic, positive or negative.

Introduction

INTRODUCTION

This workbook follows steps used in CBT.

These aim to:

- Explore the nature of the problem
- Gather information by monitoring depression levels
- Recognise the links between thoughts, emotions, physiological responses and behaviour
- Explore unhelpful thinking patterns, beliefs and behaviours
- Teach how to implement more positive and realistic thinking and reactions

These steps help us to develop healthy behaviours and thought patterns, to increase our emotional wellbeing and mental health, thereby reducing levels of anxiety.

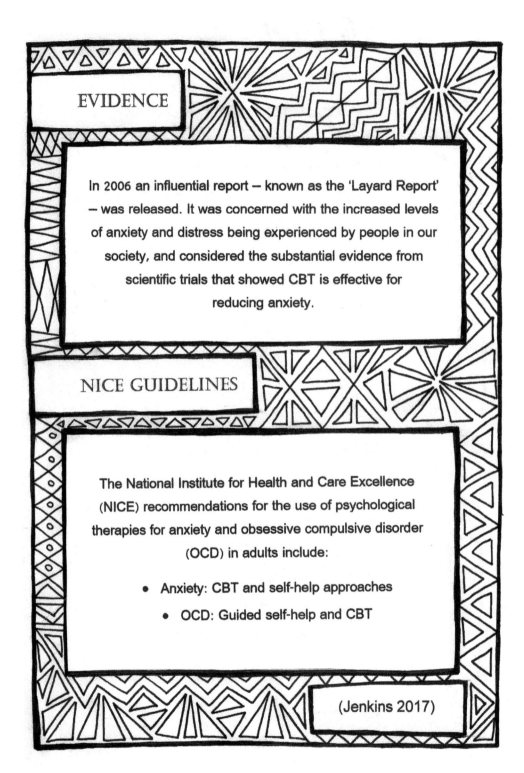

EVIDENCE

In 2006 an influential report – known as the 'Layard Report' – was released. It was concerned with the increased levels of anxiety and distress being experienced by people in our society, and considered the substantial evidence from scientific trials that showed CBT is effective for reducing anxiety.

NICE GUIDELINES

The National Institute for Health and Care Excellence (NICE) recommendations for the use of psychological therapies for anxiety and obsessive compulsive disorder (OCD) in adults include:

- Anxiety: CBT and self-help approaches
- OCD: Guided self-help and CBT

(Jenkins 2017)

WHY ART?

Having worked within the therapeutic world for nearly two decades, I consider practising therapy as a passion, alongside art-making. Expressing myself through creative means has been so profoundly therapeutic for me during times when I've experienced anxiety and stress in my life. I hope this workbook inspires you too to be creative!

If you feel comfortable about your art-making capabilities, that's great. If you're less confident, please don't let this hamper your journey with this workbook and know that the aesthetics of what you produce is not the end goal. These worksheets are about the cathartic process of creativity.

Professor Peter London would like to see a return to everyone feeling comfortable with using art-making as a means of expression, making change and identifying goals. He states in his book *No More Secondhand Art* (1989, pp.xiii–xv):

'Making images is as natural a human endeavour as speaking. The potential of carrying over from art to the transformation of a life is real – not simple or automatic, but real. The creative process is a powerful vehicle to probe what may lie ahead.'

Art therapist and author Cathy A. Malchiodi believes:

'Although there is a therapeutic benefit to expressing one's thoughts and feelings through art, one of the most impressive aspects of the art process is its potential to achieve or restore psychological equilibrium. Art can be used not only to alleviate or contain feelings of anxiety but also to repair, restore and heal.' (2007, p.134)

It doesn't matter whether your images are realistic, abstract, or a mixture of both. There's no right or wrong way to make your images. There's also the opportunity for relaxing colouring-in of the borders on every page.

Go BIG!

If you prefer to produce artwork on a larger scale please don't feel restricted to the page sizes here. You could transfer the ideas onto bigger pieces of paper or canvasses.

1

What Is Anxiety?

Shade in the most accurate statement:

ANXIETY IS
A PART OF ME

I AM
ANXIETY

ANXIETY IS A
TEMPORARY
EMOTION

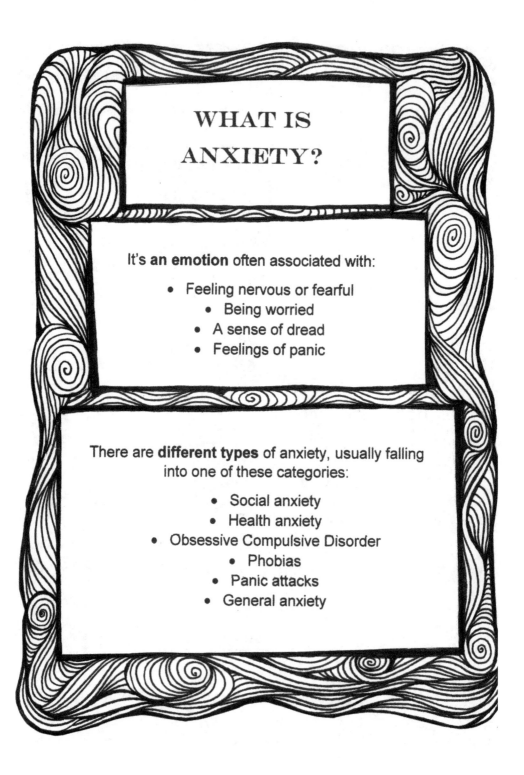

WHAT IS ANXIETY?

It's **an emotion** often associated with:

- Feeling nervous or fearful
- Being worried
- A sense of dread
- Feelings of panic

There are **different types** of anxiety, usually falling into one of these categories:

- Social anxiety
- Health anxiety
- Obsessive Compulsive Disorder
- Phobias
- Panic attacks
- General anxiety

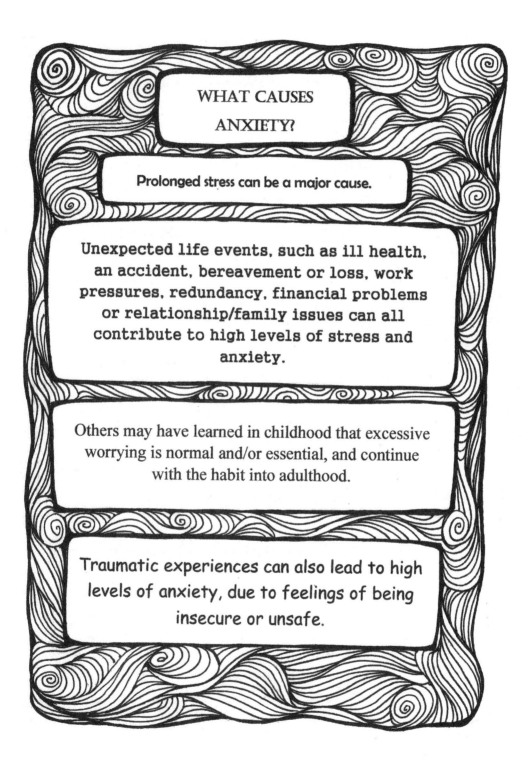

WHAT CAUSES ANXIETY?

Prolonged stress can be a major cause.

Unexpected life events, such as ill health, an accident, bereavement or loss, work pressures, redundancy, financial problems or relationship/family issues can all contribute to high levels of stress and anxiety.

Others may have learned in childhood that excessive worrying is normal and/or essential, and continue with the habit into adulthood.

Traumatic experiences can also lead to high levels of anxiety, due to feelings of being insecure or unsafe.

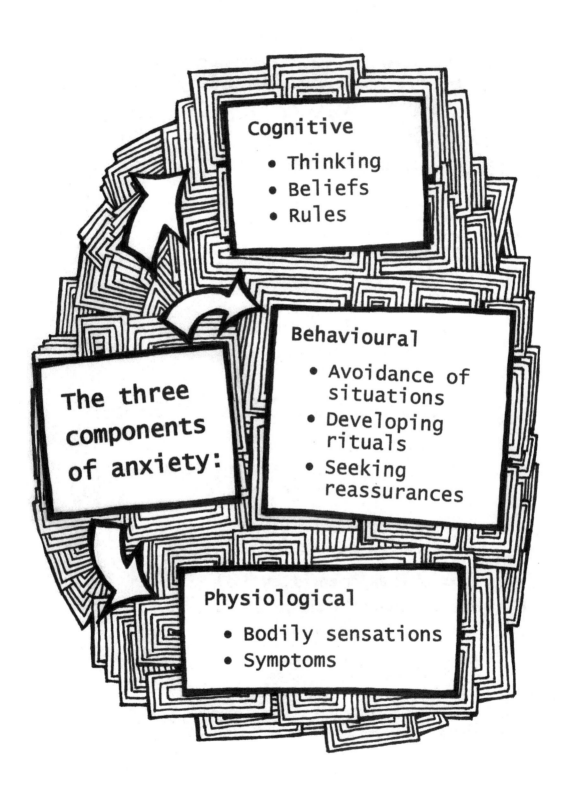

Anxious feelings

are a normal response to:

- threatening or frightening situations
- needing to deal with an emergency
- a real or perceived danger
- times/situations when we need to perform well

When we have too much stress about these situations for too long, it can lead to high levels of anxiety.

Certain thoughts – or cognitions – exacerbate anxiety, such as thinking that there is something wrong with us, or worrying we might be crazy. They can also lead to uncomfortable physical symptoms such as breathing restrictions, high blood pressure or digestive problems.

Shade in any of the boxes if you...

Often find yourself imagining the worst ☐

Have a 'whirly head' of negative thoughts ☐

Find that your sleep is affected by worries ☐

Sometimes lose your appetite, or feel sick, due to how you feel ☐

Find you have a bigger appetite than usual ☐

Feel more annoyance than usual ☐

Often have a sense of dread ☐

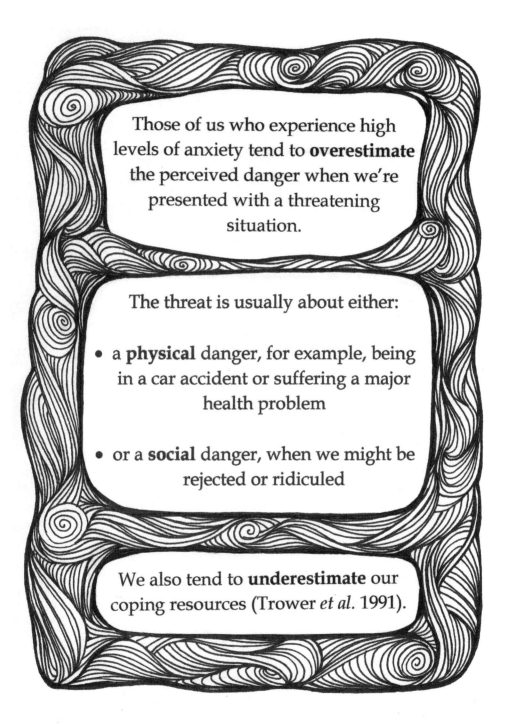

Those of us who experience high levels of anxiety tend to **overestimate** the perceived danger when we're presented with a threatening situation.

The threat is usually about either:

- a **physical** danger, for example, being in a car accident or suffering a major health problem

- or a **social** danger, when we might be rejected or ridiculed

We also tend to **underestimate** our coping resources (Trower *et al.* 1991).

2

What Is CBT?

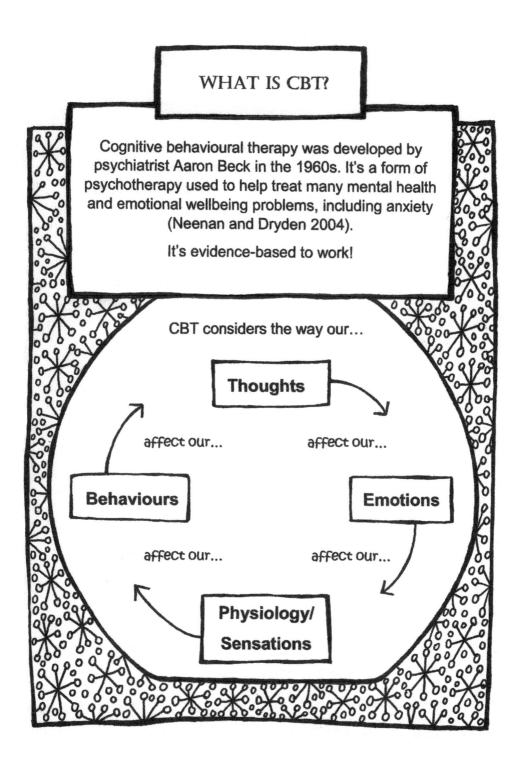

WHAT IS CBT?

Cognitive behavioural therapy was developed by psychiatrist Aaron Beck in the 1960s. It's a form of psychotherapy used to help treat many mental health and emotional wellbeing problems, including anxiety (Neenan and Dryden 2004).

It's evidence-based to work!

CBT considers the way our…

Thoughts

affect our…

affect our…

Behaviours

Emotions

affect our…

affect our…

Physiology/ Sensations

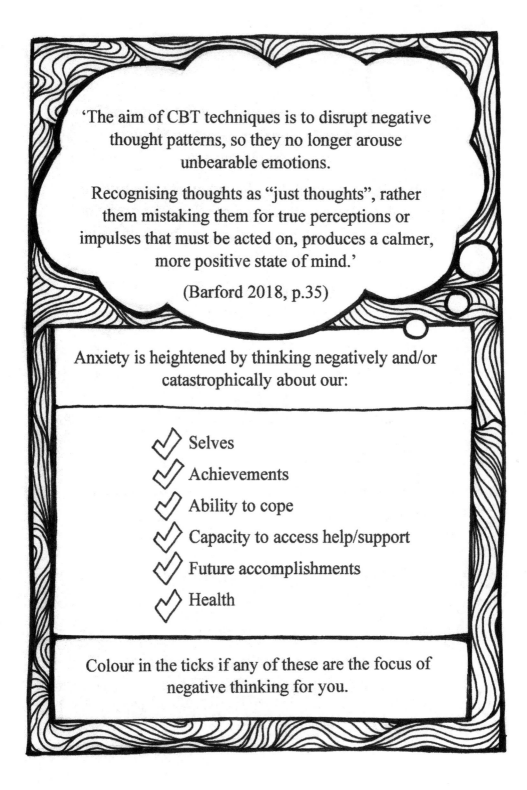

'The aim of CBT techniques is to disrupt negative thought patterns, so they no longer arouse unbearable emotions.

Recognising thoughts as "just thoughts", rather them mistaking them for true perceptions or impulses that must be acted on, produces a calmer, more positive state of mind.'

(Barford 2018, p.35)

Anxiety is heightened by thinking negatively and/or catastrophically about our:

- Selves
- Achievements
- Ability to cope
- Capacity to access help/support
- Future accomplishments
- Health

Colour in the ticks if any of these are the focus of negative thinking for you.

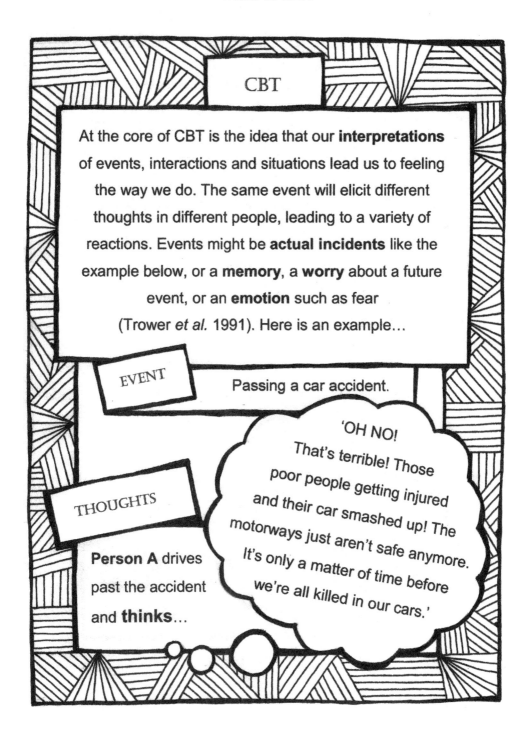

CBT

At the core of CBT is the idea that our **interpretations** of events, interactions and situations lead us to feeling the way we do. The same event will elicit different thoughts in different people, leading to a variety of reactions. Events might be **actual incidents** like the example below, or a **memory**, a **worry** about a future event, or an **emotion** such as fear (Trower *et al.* 1991). Here is an example…

EVENT

Passing a car accident.

THOUGHTS

Person A drives past the accident and **thinks**…

'OH NO! That's terrible! Those poor people getting injured and their car smashed up! The motorways just aren't safe anymore. It's only a matter of time before we're all killed in our cars.'

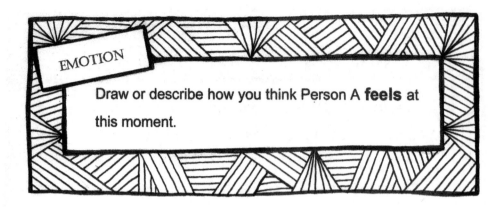

EMOTION

Draw or describe how you think Person A **feels** at this moment.

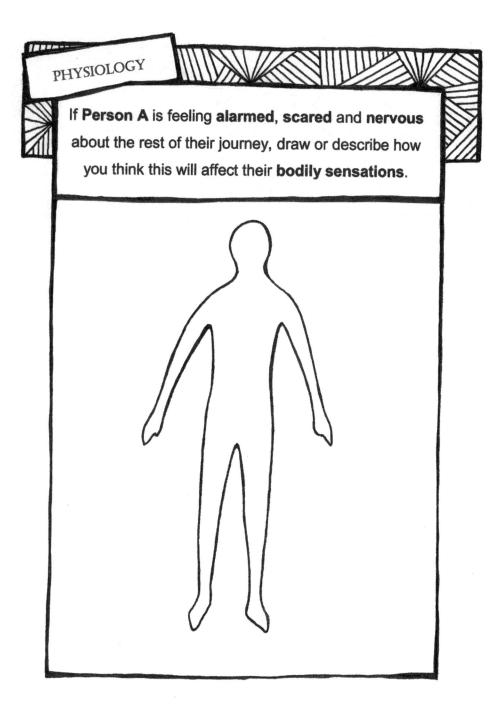

PHYSIOLOGY

If **Person A** is feeling **alarmed**, **scared** and **nervous** about the rest of their journey, draw or describe how you think this will affect their **bodily sensations**.

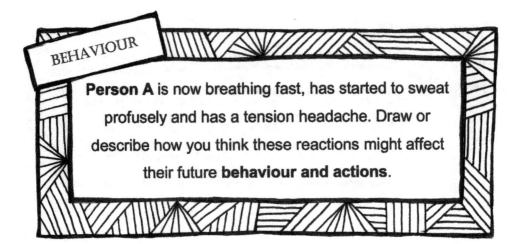

BEHAVIOUR

Person A is now breathing fast, has started to sweat profusely and has a tension headache. Draw or describe how you think these reactions might affect their future **behaviour and actions**.

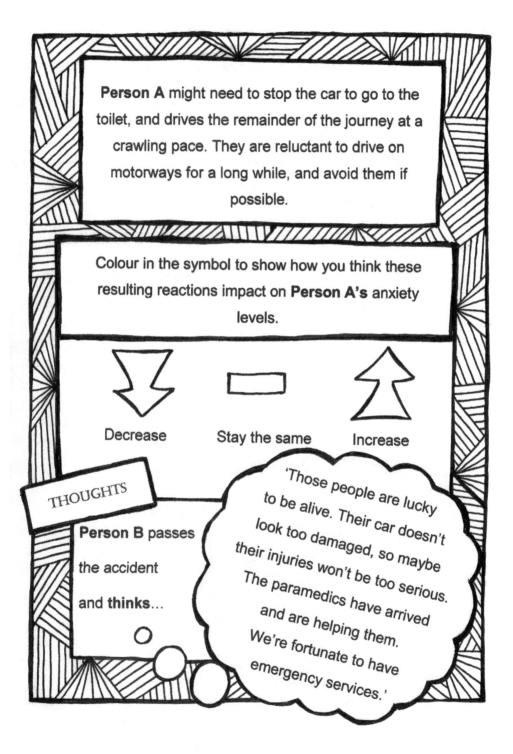

Person A might need to stop the car to go to the toilet, and drives the remainder of the journey at a crawling pace. They are reluctant to drive on motorways for a long while, and avoid them if possible.

Colour in the symbol to show how you think these resulting reactions impact on **Person A's** anxiety levels.

Decrease   Stay the same   Increase

THOUGHTS

Person B passes the accident and **thinks**…

'Those people are lucky to be alive. Their car doesn't look too damaged, so maybe their injuries won't be too serious. The paramedics have arrived and are helping them. We're fortunate to have emergency services.'

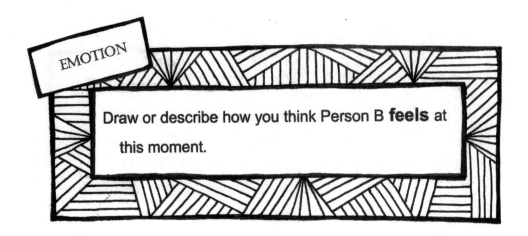

EMOTION

Draw or describe how you think Person B **feels** at this moment.

PHYSIOLOGY

If **Person B** is **feeling grateful** for the emergency services, and **relieved** that the people in the accident didn't appear to have serious injuries, draw or describe how you think these emotions will affect their **bodily sensations**.

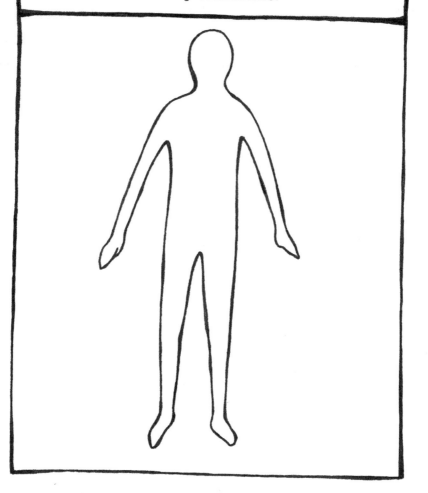

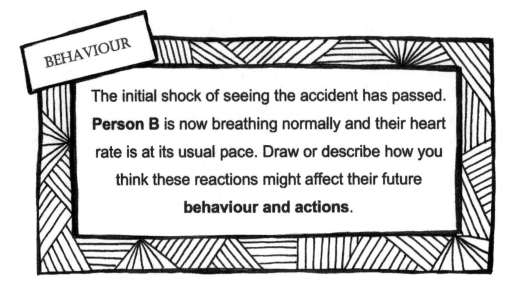

BEHAVIOUR

The initial shock of seeing the accident has passed. **Person B** is now breathing normally and their heart rate is at its usual pace. Draw or describe how you think these reactions might affect their future **behaviour and actions**.

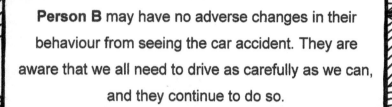

Person B may have no adverse changes in their behaviour from seeing the car accident. They are aware that we all need to drive as carefully as we can, and they continue to do so.

Colour in the symbol to show how you think these resulting reactions impact on **Person B's** anxiety levels.

Decrease

Stay the same

Increase

The EVENT witnessed by **Person A** and **Person B** is the same, yet their THOUGHTS, FEELINGS, PHYSIOLOGY, BEHAVIOUR and ANXIETY levels are different.

3

Observations

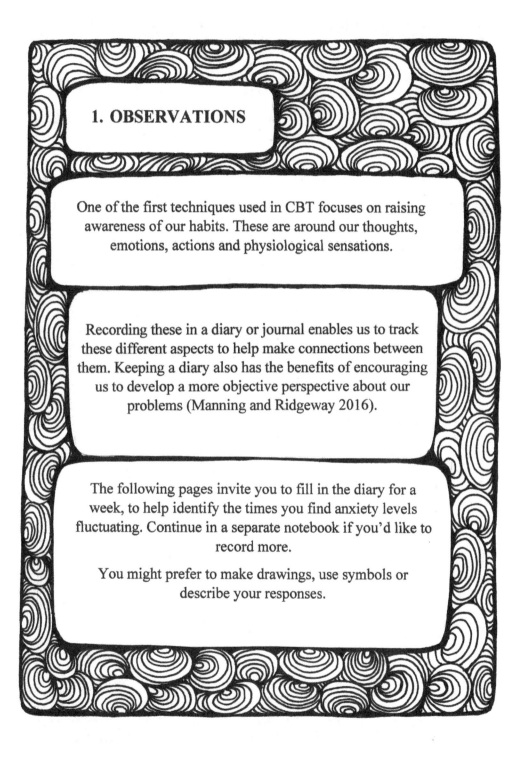

1. OBSERVATIONS

One of the first techniques used in CBT focuses on raising awareness of our habits. These are around our thoughts, emotions, actions and physiological sensations.

Recording these in a diary or journal enables us to track these different aspects to help make connections between them. Keeping a diary also has the benefits of encouraging us to develop a more objective perspective about our problems (Manning and Ridgeway 2016).

The following pages invite you to fill in the diary for a week, to help identify the times you find anxiety levels fluctuating. Continue in a separate notebook if you'd like to record more.

You might prefer to make drawings, use symbols or describe your responses.

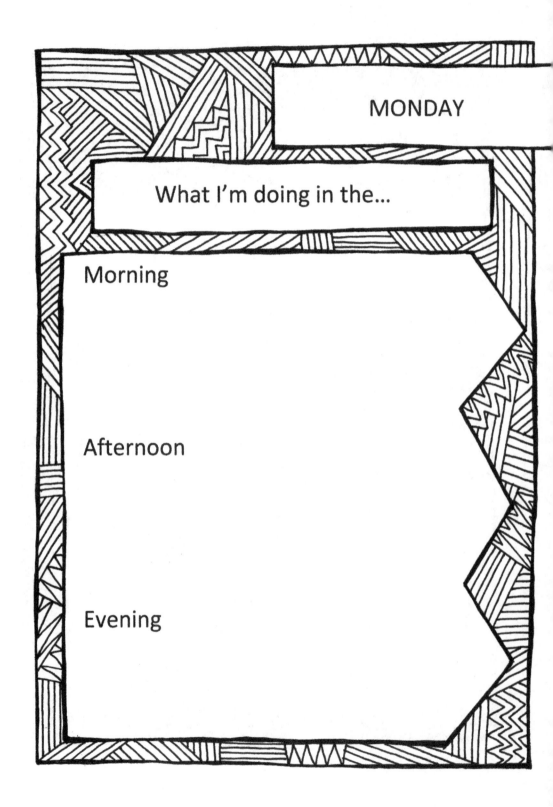

MONDAY

What I'm doing in the...

Morning

Afternoon

Evening

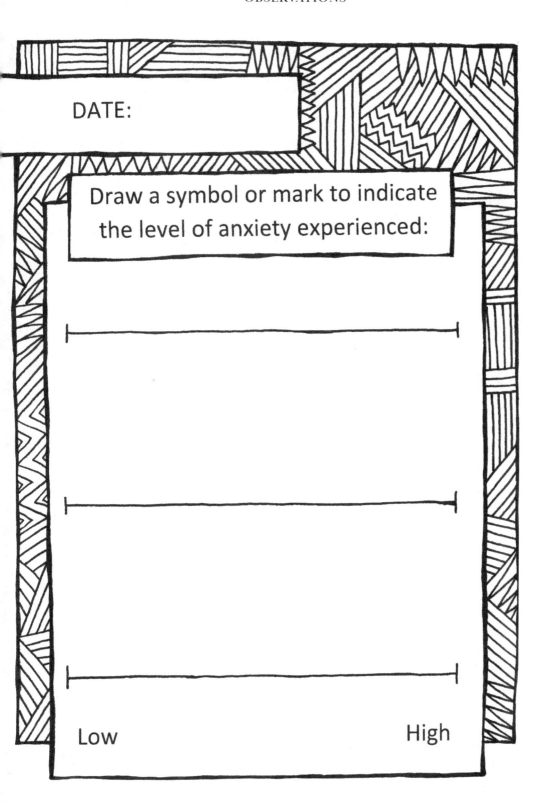

DATE:

Draw a symbol or mark to indicate the level of anxiety experienced:

Low   High

TUESDAY

What I'm doing in the...

Morning

Afternoon

Evening

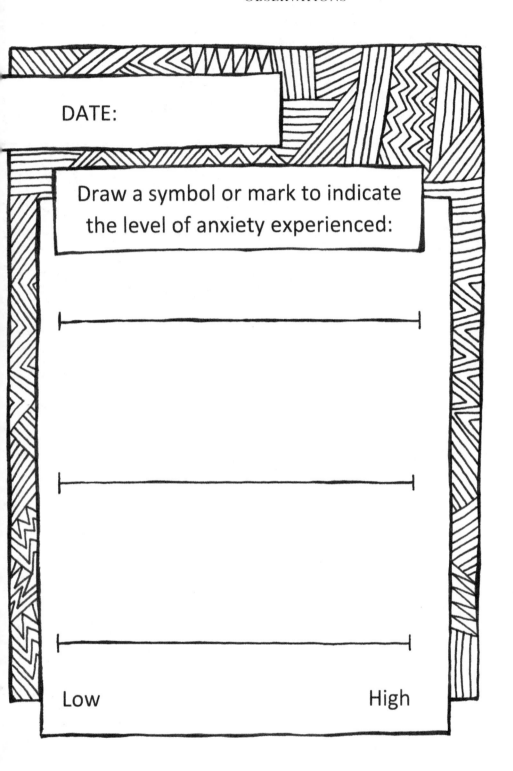

DATE:

Draw a symbol or mark to indicate
the level of anxiety experienced:

Low   High

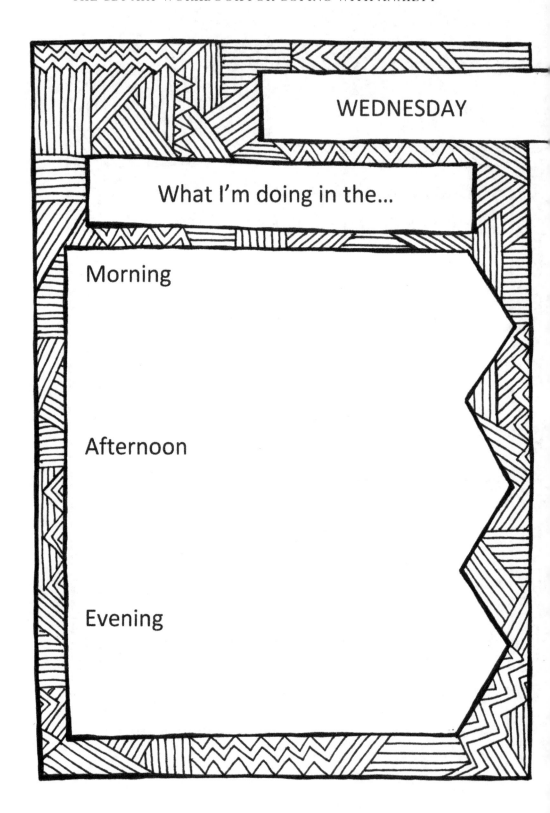

WEDNESDAY

What I'm doing in the...

Morning

Afternoon

Evening

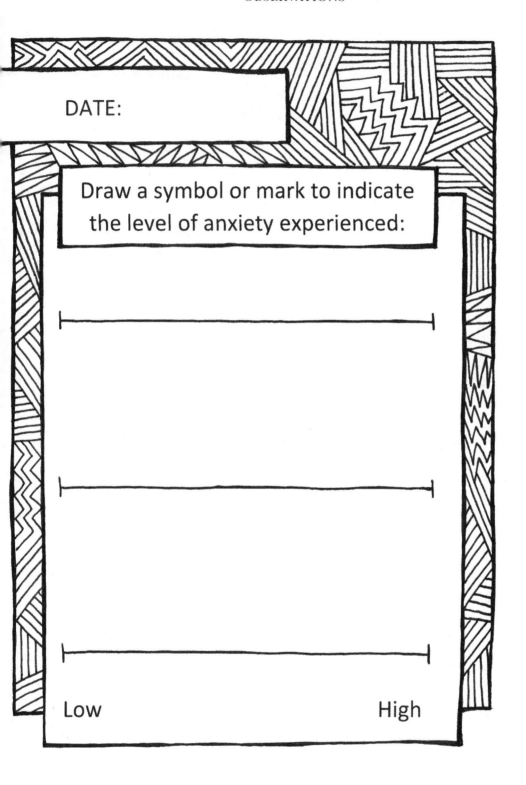

DATE:

Draw a symbol or mark to indicate the level of anxiety experienced:

Low   High

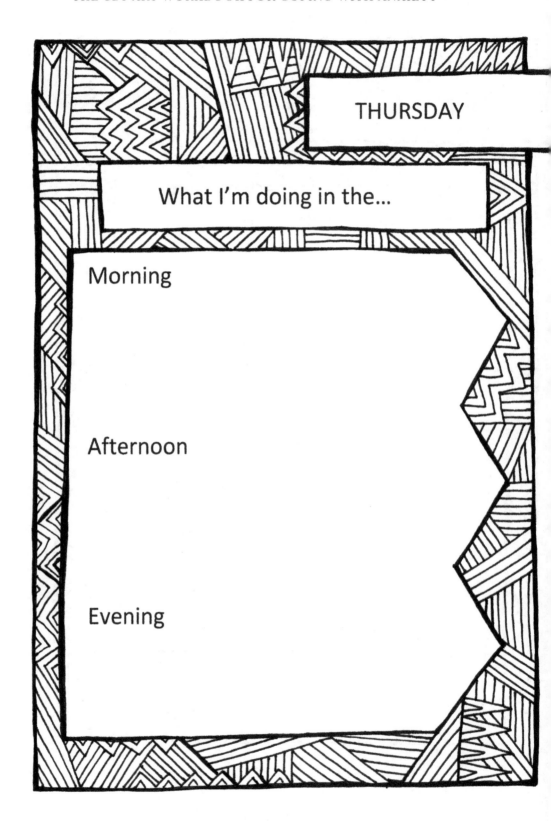

THURSDAY

What I'm doing in the...

Morning

Afternoon

Evening

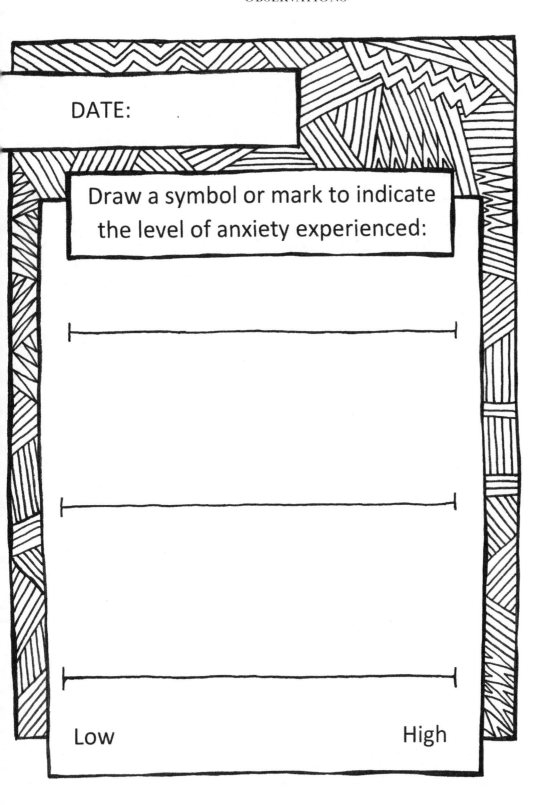

DATE:

Draw a symbol or mark to indicate
the level of anxiety experienced:

Low   High

FRIDAY

What I'm doing in the...

Morning

Afternoon

Evening

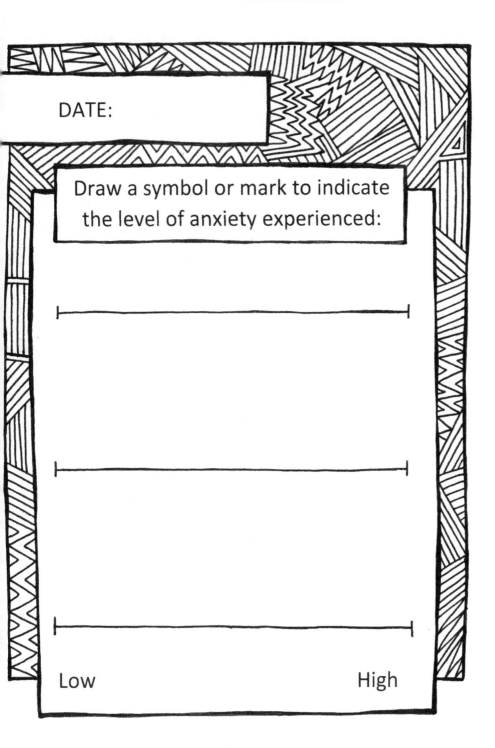

DATE:

Draw a symbol or mark to indicate the level of anxiety experienced:

Low High

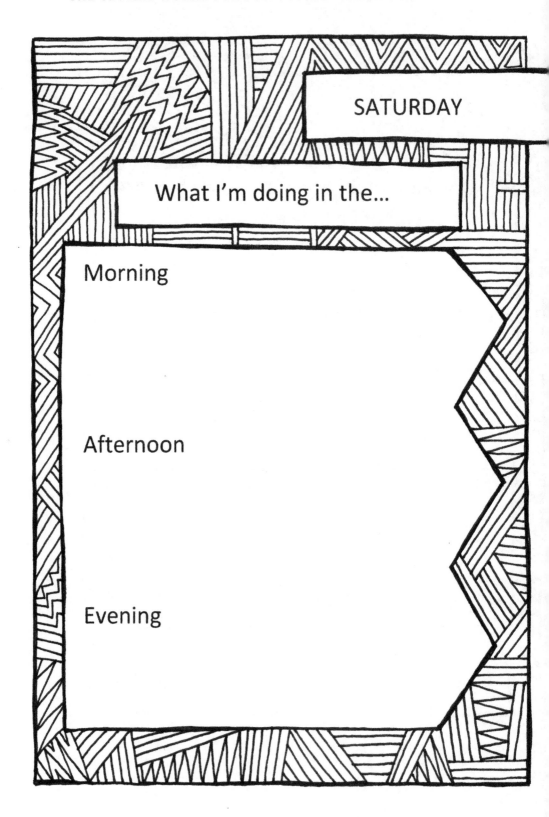

SATURDAY

What I'm doing in the...

Morning

Afternoon

Evening

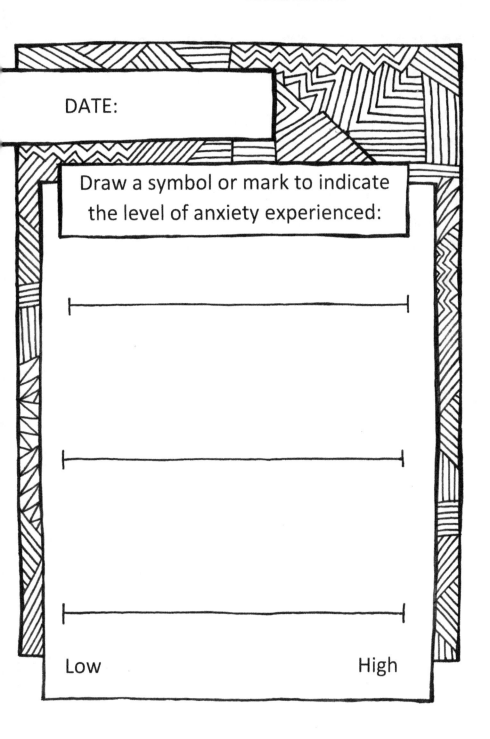

DATE:

Draw a symbol or mark to indicate
the level of anxiety experienced:

Low   High

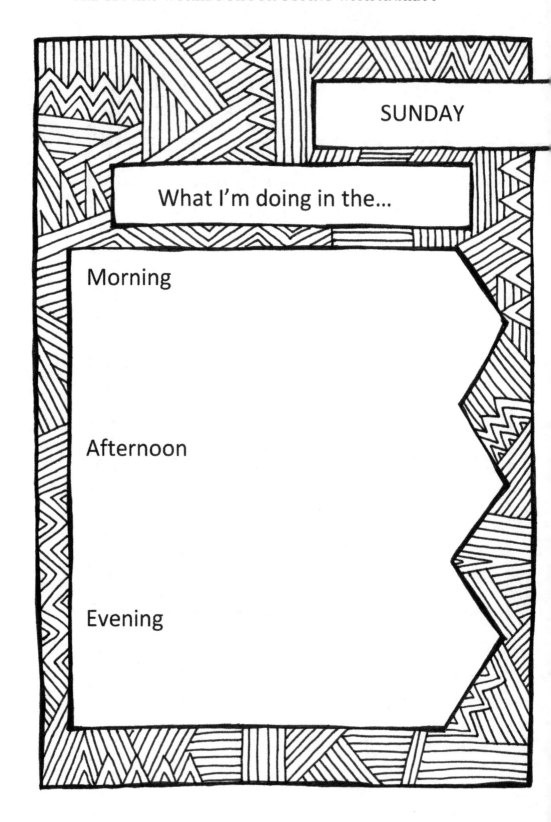

SUNDAY

What I'm doing in the...

Morning

Afternoon

Evening

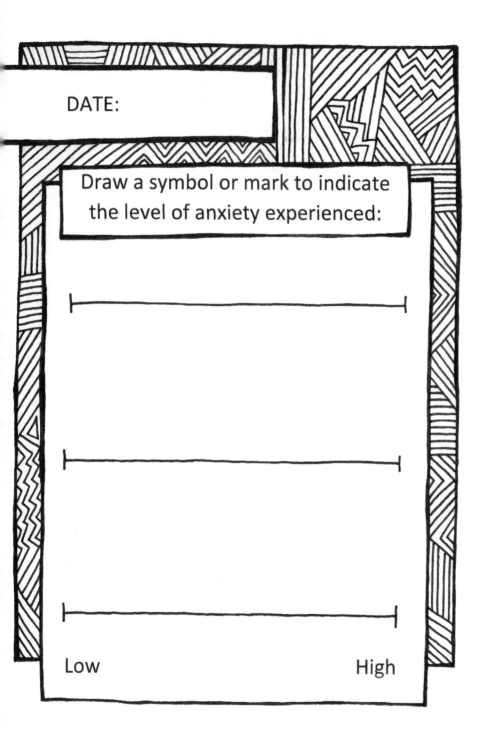

DATE:

Draw a symbol or mark to indicate
the level of anxiety experienced:

Low   High

2. OBSERVATIONS

Once we've identified some situations we find difficult, it's helpful to explore what our…

- Thoughts
- Emotions
- Physiological sensations

…were, to see how these affect our **behaviour**.

We tend to go through our usual day-to-day lives without being very much aware of what our thoughts are about specific things, and how our thinking affects our emotions, mood and behaviour.

Recording some of these helps us to focus on what we want to change, and makes us realise that we can have more control over our emotional and behavioural reactions.

Fill in the following pages with some of the situations when you notice you experience anxiety.

Day   Date

1. Draw or describe the situation/trigger:

What were your thoughts?

What were your
emotions?

Place a colour
next to each one:

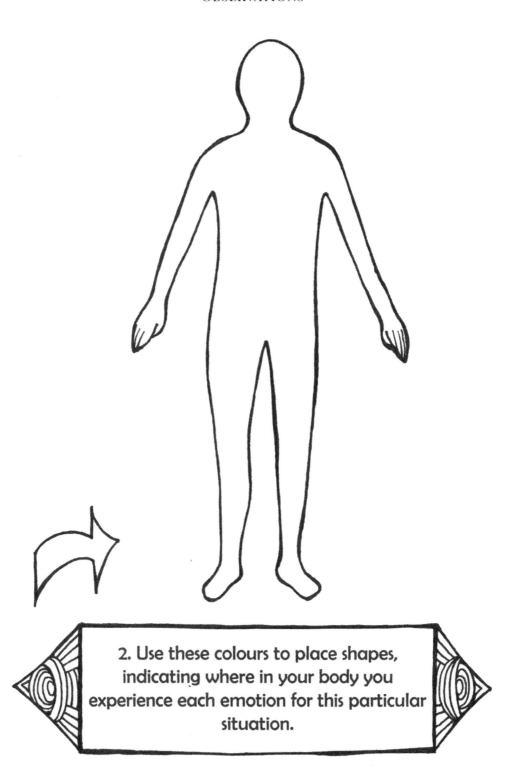

2. Use these colours to place shapes, indicating where in your body you experience each emotion for this particular situation.

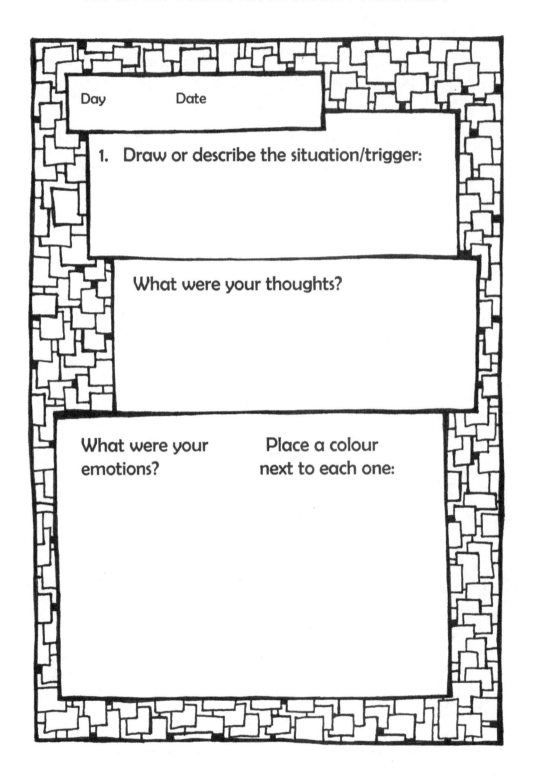

Day   Date

1. Draw or describe the situation/trigger:

What were your thoughts?

What were your   Place a colour
emotions?   next to each one:

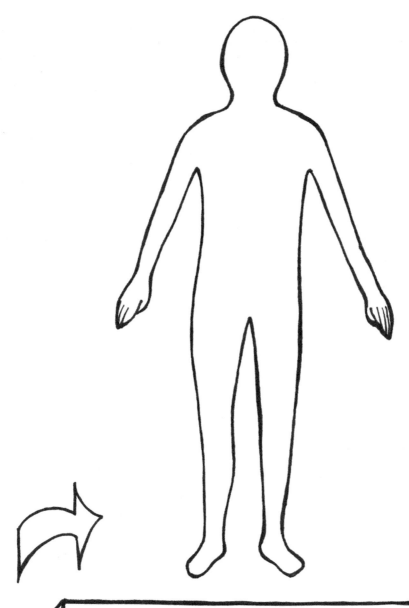

2. Use these colours to place shapes, indicating where in your body you experience each emotion for this particular situation.

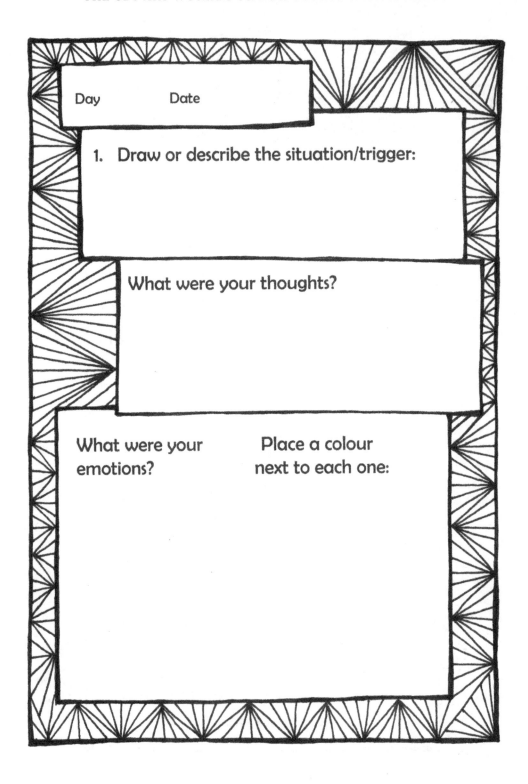

Day   Date

1. Draw or describe the situation/trigger:

What were your thoughts?

What were your   Place a colour
emotions?   next to each one:

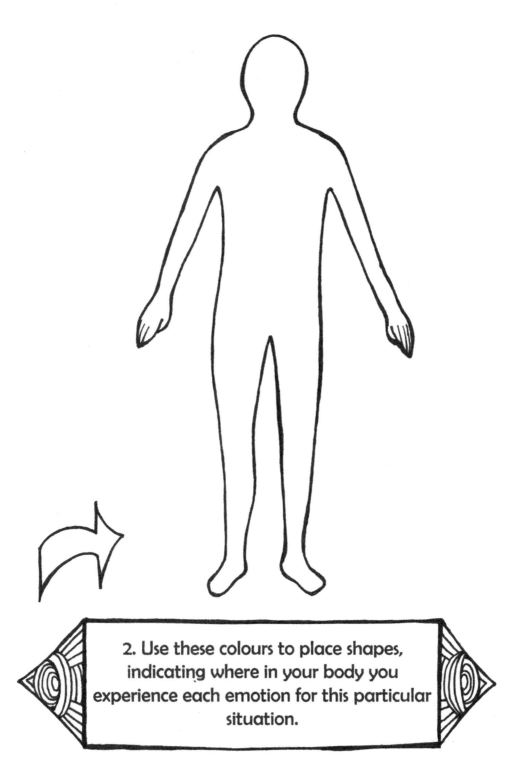

2. Use these colours to place shapes, indicating where in your body you experience each emotion for this particular situation.

4

Cognitions

Cognitions

The level of anxiety we experience is predominantly influenced by two things:

- How threatening we believe the situation is

- How confident we feel in our ability to cope with the situation

(Trower *et al.* 1991)

By exploring what our thoughts are, we can acknowledge and understand how these can have a negative impact, by how they:

- Exacerbate our perceptions of the threat

- Lower our confidence and belief in ourselves that we can deal with the threat

The worksheet pages in this chapter invite you to explore your thinking, to identify which thoughts increase anxiety levels and which are calming and soothing.

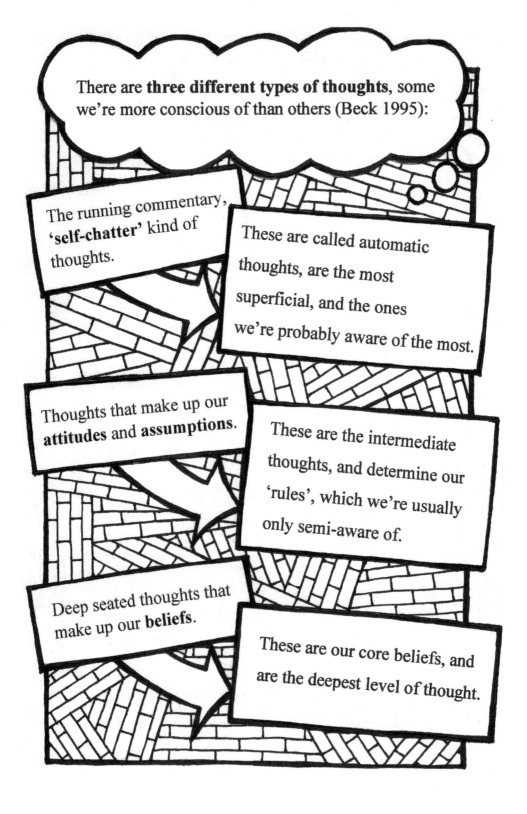

There are **three different types of thoughts**, some we're more conscious of than others (Beck 1995):

The running commentary, **'self-chatter'** kind of thoughts.

These are called automatic thoughts, are the most superficial, and the ones we're probably aware of the most.

Thoughts that make up our **attitudes** and **assumptions**.

These are the intermediate thoughts, and determine our 'rules', which we're usually only semi-aware of.

Deep seated thoughts that make up our **beliefs**.

These are our core beliefs, and are the deepest level of thought.

It's usual in CBT to look at the automatic thoughts first, to become aware of the nature of our inner talk.

Draw a symbol on the scale to indicate how your self-chatter generally is:

Kind ⊢———————————————————⊣ Critical

The following pages invite you to have a look at your thoughts in more depth, in order to identify where changes can be made to help you feel calmer.

To explore and practise new ways of thinking can feel like a venture into the unknown, and scary. Stick with trying to make these changes and you'll soon see the benefits of feeling more empowered and less anxious!

The following pages show some **self-soothing affirmations.**

Affirmations are positive statements. As soon as you notice your inner self-talk becoming negative or critical, replace it with an affirmation, such as the ones on the next few pages.

Try repeating the affirmations over and over in your mind as you colour in the phrase. The more often you practise, the easier it will be to remember them and you'll be able to more readily access them in future situations to help halt rising anxiety.

Ideally these will start to develop into your beliefs.

The more familiar you become with positive thoughts and how they feel, the sooner you'll notice when your thoughts are not soothing or nurturing.

Attitudes and Assumptions

When certain automatic thoughts become habitual, they can develop into our attitudes and assumptions. Draw or describe any negative views you have about...

WORK

Boss

Colleagues

Workload

Income

Career

Studies

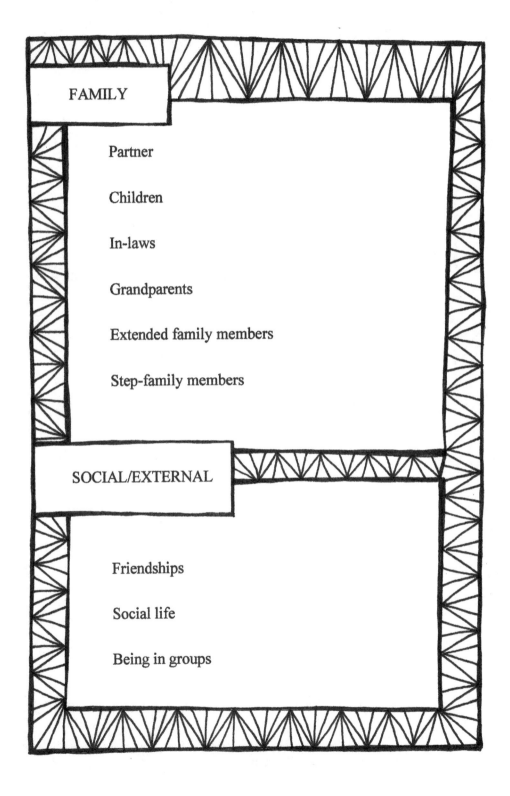

FAMILY

Partner

Children

In-laws

Grandparents

Extended family members

Step-family members

SOCIAL/EXTERNAL

Friendships

Social life

Being in groups

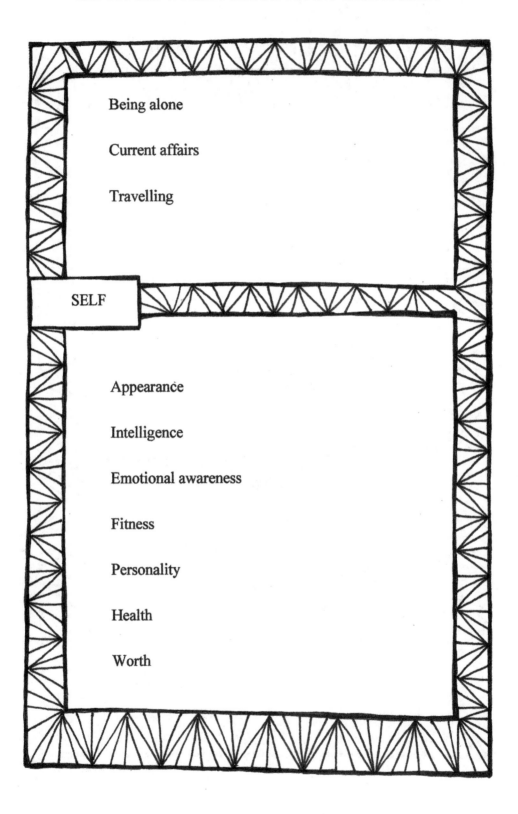

Being alone

Current affairs

Travelling

SELF

Appearance

Intelligence

Emotional awareness

Fitness

Personality

Health

Worth

1. It's helpful to question where our negative assumptions and attitudes have come from...

EXAMPLE

Let's use the example of a boss you feel highly anxious around. If your two previous bosses have been ruthless tyrants, you may have the view that all bosses behave this way, and you may be nervously waiting for your current boss to become ruthless and harsh.

- How much evidence is there to support your view that your current boss will behave like your previous ones?

- Is it realistic or selective?

'In all anxiety problems, there is a tendency...to overestimate the probability of bad things occurring and to catastrophise about the consequences of this predicted bad event.

[There is]...the tendency to be hypersensitive to the threatening aspects of the situation and ignore the positive or benign.'

(Trower *et al.* 1991, p.110)

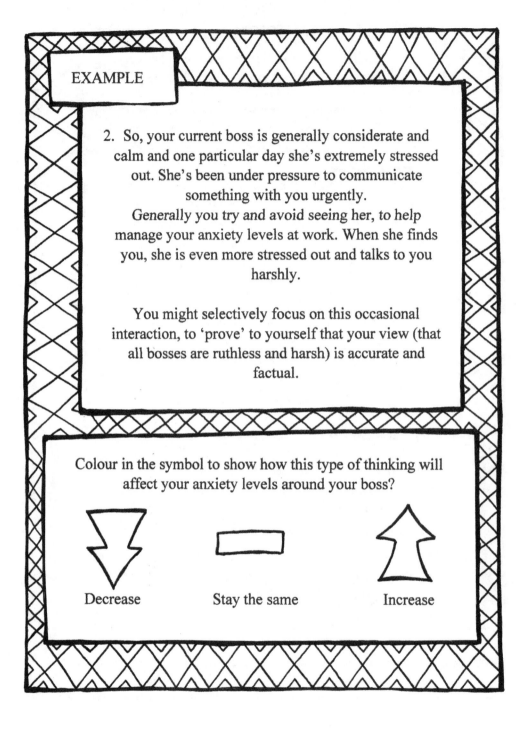

EXAMPLE

2. So, your current boss is generally considerate and calm and one particular day she's extremely stressed out. She's been under pressure to communicate something with you urgently.
Generally you try and avoid seeing her, to help manage your anxiety levels at work. When she finds you, she is even more stressed out and talks to you harshly.

You might selectively focus on this occasional interaction, to 'prove' to yourself that your view (that all bosses are ruthless and harsh) is accurate and factual.

Colour in the symbol to show how this type of thinking will affect your anxiety levels around your boss?

Decrease   Stay the same   Increase

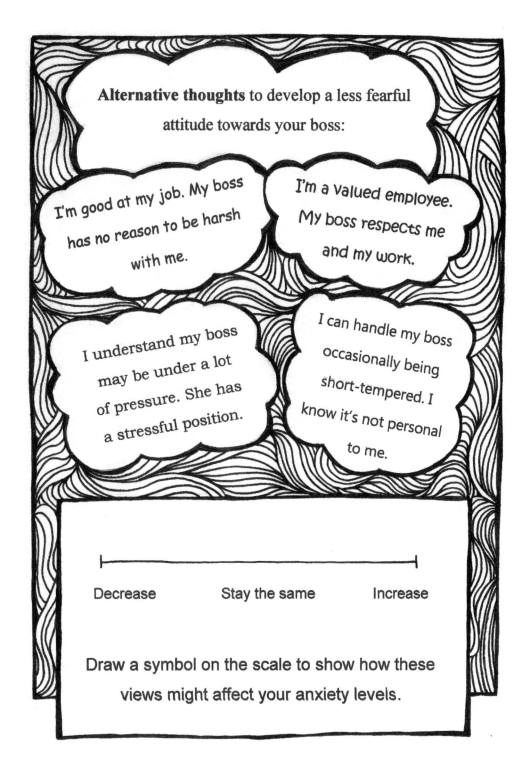

Alternative thoughts to develop a less fearful attitude towards your boss:

I'm good at my job. My boss has no reason to be harsh with me.

I'm a valued employee. My boss respects me and my work.

I understand my boss may be under a lot of pressure. She has a stressful position.

I can handle my boss occasionally being short-tempered. I know it's not personal to me.

Decrease   Stay the same   Increase

Draw a symbol on the scale to show how these views might affect your anxiety levels.

Beliefs

It's helpful to explore our underlying beliefs to try and identify if these are impacting negatively on our emotional state.

1. Colour in the crosses if you have any of these kinds of beliefs:

I *must* do well and win people's approval or else I am worthless.

Other people *must* treat me considerately and kindly, in exactly the way I want them to (otherwise, they can be blamed).

Life must give me all that I want quickly and easily, and give me nothing that I don't want.

(Ellis 1977)

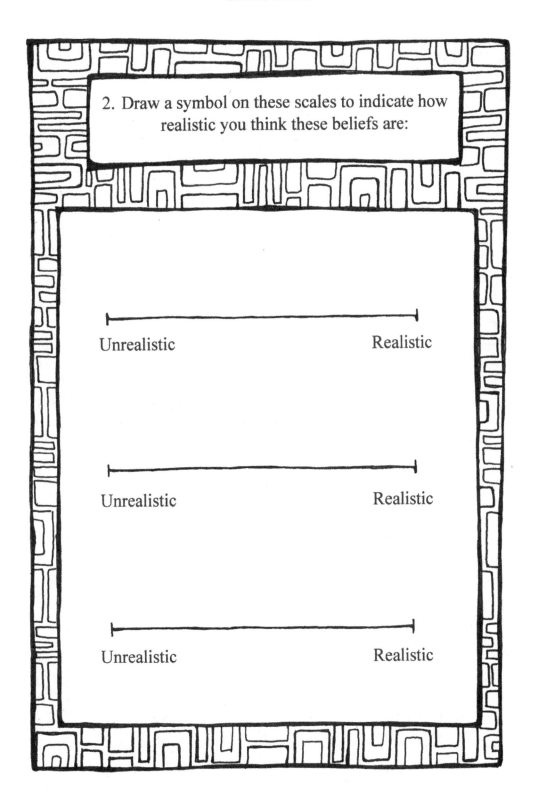

2. Draw a symbol on these scales to indicate how realistic you think these beliefs are:

Unrealistic   Realistic

Unrealistic   Realistic

Unrealistic   Realistic

Think of some healthier beliefs you could start to develop, which will not increase anxiety levels. Here are two examples:

Not everyone is going to like me, and that's okay

I cope well with life's challenges

1. Anxiety Creature

How would anxiety look if it were a creature?

You could also create this image on a separate piece of paper which you could then scrunch up into a tight ball, and throw out, or rip the paper into shreds.

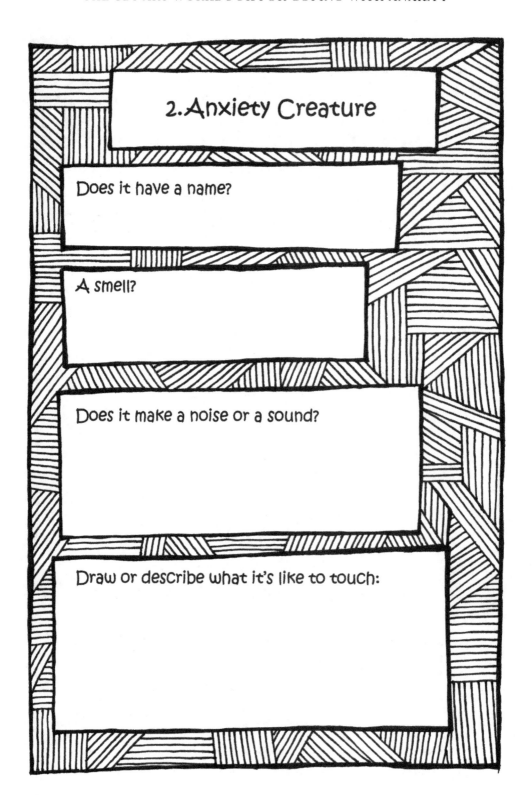

2.Anxiety Creature

Does it have a name?

A smell?

Does it make a noise or a sound?

Draw or describe what it's like to touch:

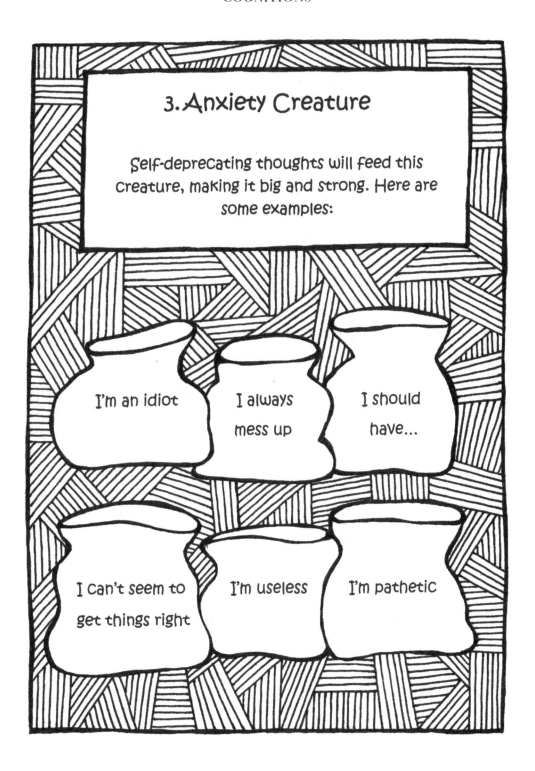

3. Anxiety Creature

Self-deprecating thoughts will feed this creature, making it big and strong. Here are some examples:

I'm an idiot

I always mess up

I should have...

I can't seem to get things right

I'm useless

I'm pathetic

4. Anxiety Creature

What kinds of negative thoughts feed your anxiety creature, making it strong and big?

5. Anxiety Creature

On the other hand, some thoughts will starve this creature, making it weaker and smaller. Affirmations will help to shrink anxiety!

I'm a good person

I did as well as I could

I handled it okay

I am safe

I'm doing my best

My feelings are important

Everything's going to be alright

6. Anxiety Creature

What affirmations will shrink your anxiety Creature?

It's helpful to repeat these many, many times a day in your mind. Then when you notice the negative thoughts creeping in to feed the anxiety creature, you will be more practised at using these affirmations to begin to starve it.

Your Mind as a Garden

Another way of considering thoughts is to imagine that your mind is like a garden.

Unwanted, negative and critical thoughts are like weeds. These can dominate and strangle the flowers which are our positive and nourishing thoughts. We can choose to allow the weeds to come into our garden and take over, or we can be more proactive about what we allow into our minds, and help protect the flowers that we want to keep alive.

The weeds will keep coming back if we let them! We need to be vigilant about what thoughts we let in and nourish.

This gets easier with practice, and the first step is noticing what our thoughts are and how they make us feel, to identify which are the weeds and which are the flowers.

How would you draw or paint your mind, as a garden?

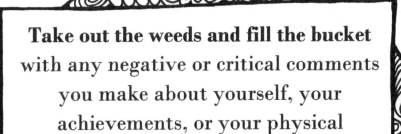

Take out the weeds and fill the bucket with any negative or critical comments you make about yourself, your achievements, or your physical appearance.

Once the negative thoughts are in the bucket, paint over them or cross them out.

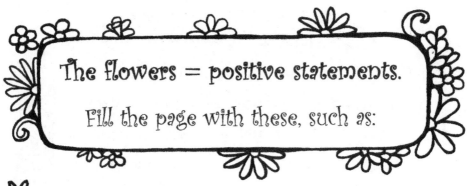

The flowers = positive statements.

Fill the page with these, such as:

I'm a good friend

I handled it as best I could

I'm kind

I'm a loving person

5

Emotions

EMOTIONS

Draw a symbol on the scale to show how comfortable you are with emotions like anxiety?

Relaxed   Uncomfortable

Most of us develop strategies (often without realising we're doing it) to deal with difficult emotions which feel uncomfortable, but over time this can cause an increase in intensity in those emotions.

The more you begin to practise staying with your feelings, **the less you will fear them.**

Beliefs about emotions

You can only start to **take control** of your emotions if you **believe that you can,** and this is essential for lowering emotional distress.

(Winch 2018)

Draw a symbol on the scale to show whether you believe your emotions are fixed or malleable?

|————————————————————————|

Fixed   Malleable

'Beliefs that individuals hold about whether emotions are malleable or fixed may play a crucial role in individuals' emotional experiences and their engagement in changing their emotions.'

(Kneeland *et al.* 2016, pp.81-88)

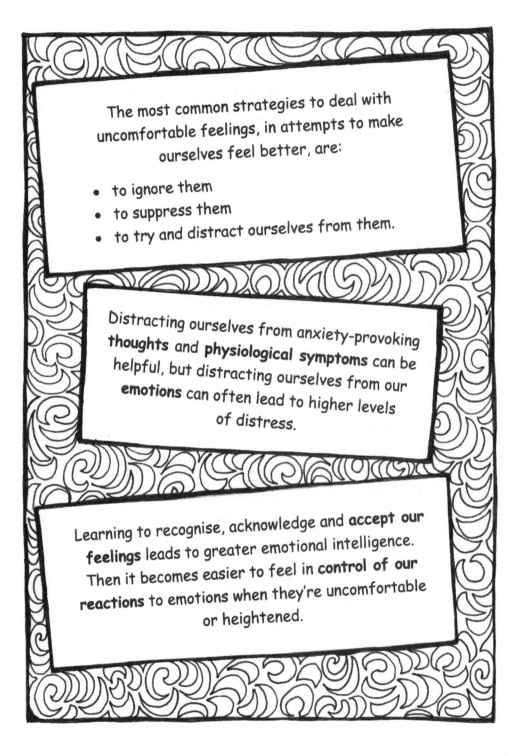

The most common strategies to deal with uncomfortable feelings, in attempts to make ourselves feel better, are:

- to ignore them
- to suppress them
- to try and distract ourselves from them.

Distracting ourselves from anxiety-provoking **thoughts** and **physiological symptoms** can be helpful, but distracting ourselves from our **emotions** can often lead to higher levels of distress.

Learning to recognise, acknowledge and **accept our feelings** leads to greater emotional intelligence. Then it becomes easier to feel in **control of our reactions** to emotions when they're uncomfortable or heightened.

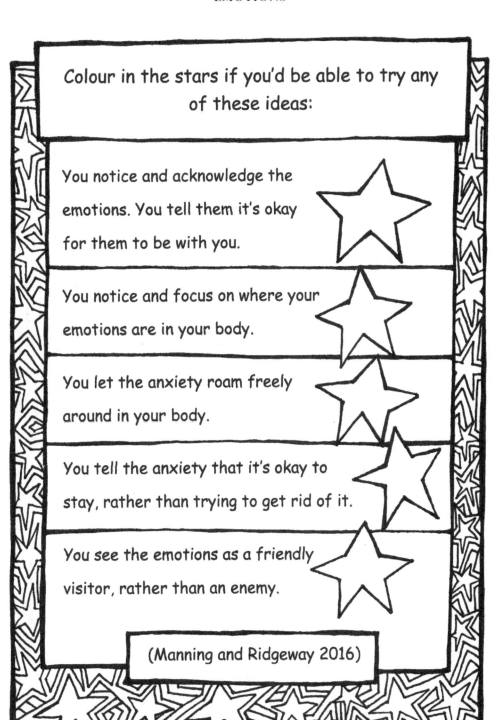

Colour in the stars if you'd be able to try any of these ideas:

You notice and acknowledge the emotions. You tell them it's okay for them to be with you.

You notice and focus on where your emotions are in your body.

You let the anxiety roam freely around in your body.

You tell the anxiety that it's okay to stay, rather than trying to get rid of it.

You see the emotions as a friendly visitor, rather than an enemy.

(Manning and Ridgeway 2016)

Journalling

Mercer et al. (2010) discovered that medical students were experiencing higher levels of stress and anxiety than the average population, and carried out a study. This demonstrated how visual journalling was helpful for reducing stress and anxiety levels.

Creating a visual journal can be a great release for emotional expression. On the following pages, begin a journal to express your feelings for each day. Draw an image to represent your emotions with no other agenda than to help you connect with your emotional world, express these emotions and release them.
Continue this practice in a separate notebook if you find it therapeutic.

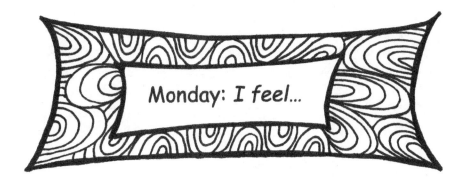

Monday: *I feel...*

Tuesday: *I feel...*

Wednesday: *I feel...*

Thursday: *I feel...*

Friday: *I feel...*

Sunday: *I feel...*

Acceptance
of anxious feelings

Draw an image of what this looks like for you:

6

Physiology

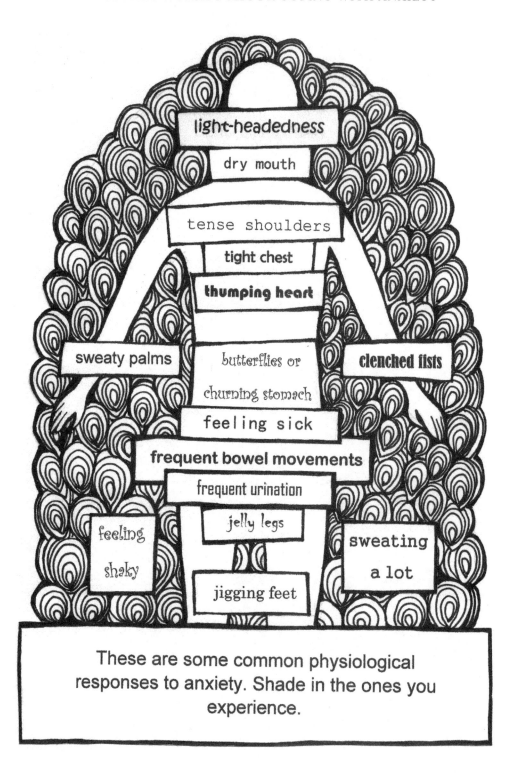

light-headedness

dry mouth

tense shoulders

tight chest

thumping heart

sweaty palms

butterflies or churning stomach

clenched fists

feeling sick

frequent bowel movements

frequent urination

jelly legs

feeling shaky

sweating a lot

jigging feet

These are some common physiological responses to anxiety. Shade in the ones you experience.

PHYSIOLOGY

Distraction techniques are useful for taking our mind away from physiological symptoms of anxiety, and as a result the symptoms can disappear. Draw or describe this sensory perceptions technique:

5 things I can see:

4 things I can touch:

3 things I can hear:

2 things I can smell:

1 thing I can taste:

1 good thing about ME:

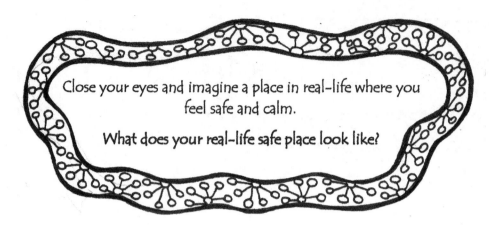

Close your eyes and imagine a place in real-life where you feel safe and calm.

What does your real-life safe place look like?

Close your eyes and picture an imaginary place where you feel safe and calm.

What does your imaginary safe place look like?

7

Behaviours

BEHAVIOURS

Colour in the ticks if you do some of these common **behaviours** when it comes to high anxiety levels:

ESCAPE

If escaping situations becomes habitual, it can perpetuate the belief that anxiety will become overwhelming if you stay.

AVOIDANCE

This usually offers only short-term relief as it can then lower confidence levels in your ability to cope.

SAFETY BEHAVIOURS

These can involve making numerous checks. They also offer only short-term relief and can exacerbate anxiety in the long run.

ALCOHOL CONSUMPTION

At the time alcohol can temporarily dampen feelings of anxiety, but the following day anxiety is often exacerbated.

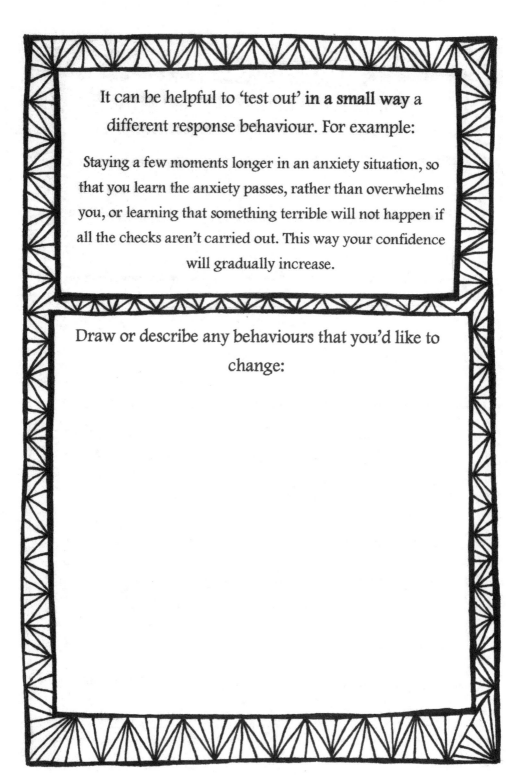

It can be helpful to 'test out' **in a small way** a different response behaviour. For example:

Staying a few moments longer in an anxiety situation, so that you learn the anxiety passes, rather than overwhelms you, or learning that something terrible will not happen if all the checks aren't carried out. This way your confidence will gradually increase.

Draw or describe any behaviours that you'd like to change:

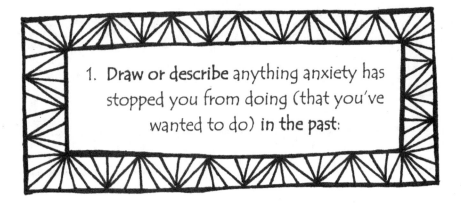

1. **Draw or describe** anything anxiety has stopped you from doing (that you've wanted to do) **in the past:**

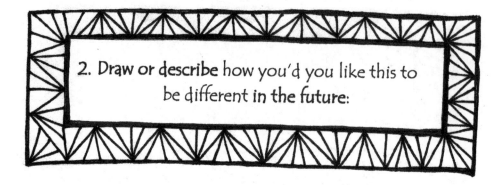

2. Draw or describe how you'd you like this to be different in the future:

8

Different Types of Anxiety

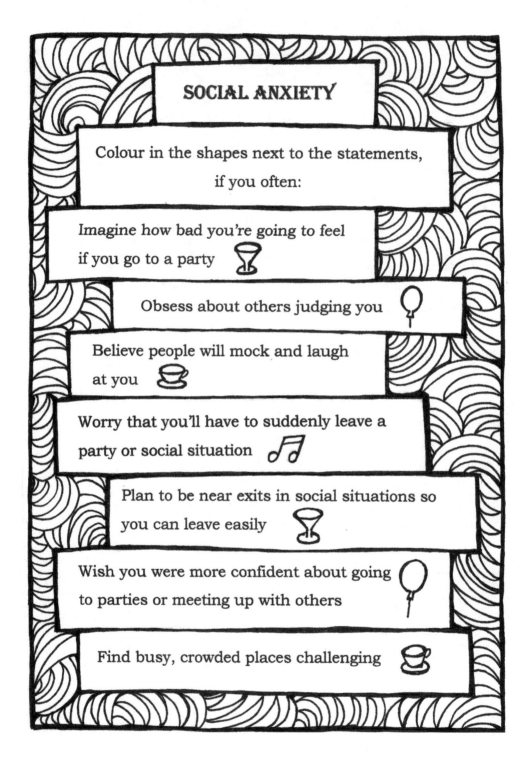

SOCIAL ANXIETY

Colour in the shapes next to the statements, if you often:

Imagine how bad you're going to feel if you go to a party

Obsess about others judging you

Believe people will mock and laugh at you

Worry that you'll have to suddenly leave a party or social situation

Plan to be near exits in social situations so you can leave easily

Wish you were more confident about going to parties or meeting up with others

Find busy, crowded places challenging

Making Comparisons

Jenkins (2017, p.22) writes about how Wilkinson and Pickett (2010) believe that high levels of social anxiety are caused by social inequality, as this increases 'a sense of social evaluative threat'. They noted how lower levels of mental health problems were reported in more equal societies.

They suggest it's the way in which

we compare our...

- Behaviour
- Achievements
- Possessions

...with those of others that leads to this 'social evaluative threat'.

Increasing our confidence through practising replacing critical thoughts with **affirmations** can really help to reduce social anxiety.

This will then impact on our **attitudes and assumptions**. We can start to think that it doesn't matter if someone is inconsiderate or judges us, and we **will cope** with the situation if they do!

Nobody *actually* died of embarrassment. If we're feeling like an idiot over something we did, we need to give ourselves a break by replacing the critical self-talk with kind and nourishing words.

Our **beliefs** need to let us make a mistake once in a while. The pressure to get everything right all the time isn't healthy, and is probably more likely to lead us to being more anxious and making a mistake.

Making small changes that gradually take us out of our comfort zone can boost our **confidence** that **nothing bad will happen**, and over time will lead us to reaching our goals.

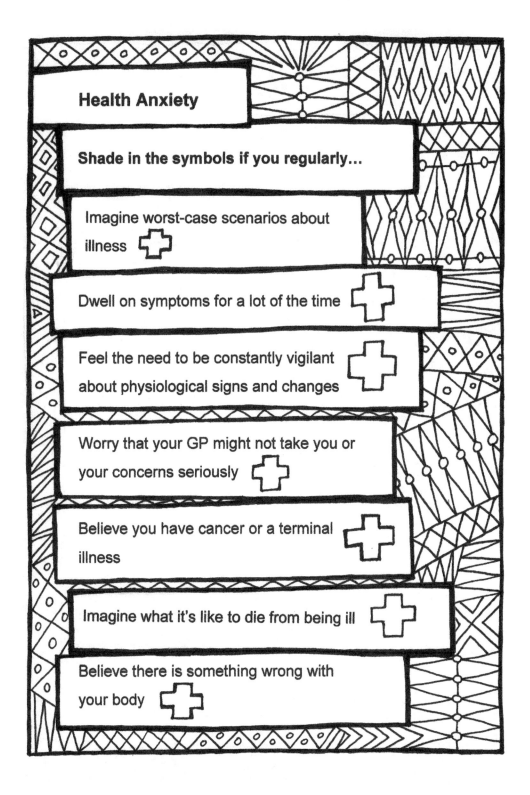

Health Anxiety

Shade in the symbols if you regularly…

Imagine worst-case scenarios about illness

Dwell on symptoms for a lot of the time

Feel the need to be constantly vigilant about physiological signs and changes

Worry that your GP might not take you or your concerns seriously

Believe you have cancer or a terminal illness

Imagine what it's like to die from being ill

Believe there is something wrong with your body

Body checking

If you're currently checking your body several times a day, this can have a debilitating effect on your daily life. The check often provides only momentary relief from worry and can increase anxiety levels.

Think up a symbol for your checks and draw these to show how many times per day in a week you feel the need to check.

Monday

Tuesday

Wednesday

Thursday

Friday

Saturday

Sunday

Take notice if there are any days when the number is more or less. Why is this?

You are IN CONTROL of how many times you check your body!

If your goal is to check your body just twice a day (or less), what would be the worst-case, realistic scenario of missing a lump, bump, scratch or blemish for half a day? Catastrophising over every changing bodily sensation or symptom can become a habit. Try and notice your thoughts when you do this.

How many are realistic and how many are catastrophic?

Reducing the number of checks can REDUCE anxiety levels!

You could make a plan to gradually reduce the number of checks over a few days. Draw a picture of you feeling comfortable with only checking twice a day (or less).

Paradoxical ideas

Shade over any of these statements you'd like to become true:

'I'd like to alienate all my family and friends with always talking about my health worries and showing little interest in their lives.'

'I would like to spend lots of my future time attending medical appointments for the rest of my life.'

'I'd love to spend every day, for the rest of my life, thinking about dying and what this will be like.'

'I'd like to think about, and do nothing else in my life, apart from focusing on bodily symptoms and changes.'

'I'm looking forward to spending my remaining time on earth in a constant state of stress, worrying about my body.'

'I would love to be tested again and again, for every possible disease and serious illness there is known to humans.'

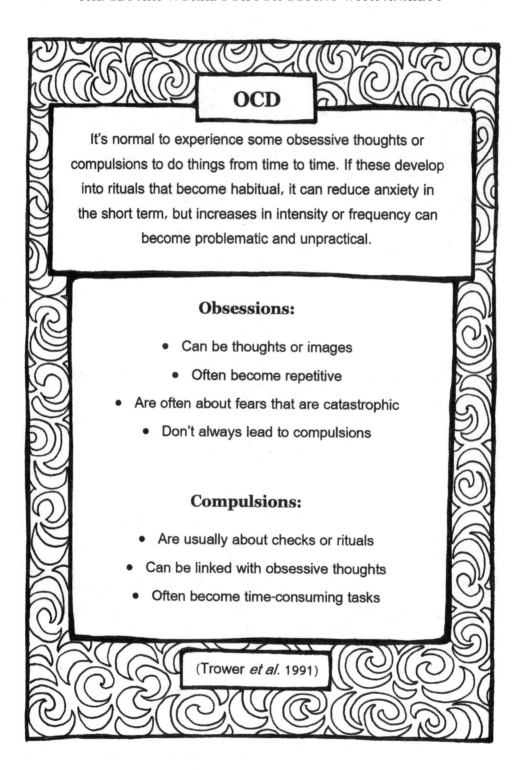

OCD

It's normal to experience some obsessive thoughts or compulsions to do things from time to time. If these develop into rituals that become habitual, it can reduce anxiety in the short term, but increases in intensity or frequency can become problematic and unpractical.

Obsessions:

- Can be thoughts or images
- Often become repetitive
- Are often about fears that are catastrophic
- Don't always lead to compulsions

Compulsions:

- Are usually about checks or rituals
- Can be linked with obsessive thoughts
- Often become time-consuming tasks

(Trower *et al.* 1991)

It can be helpful to remind ourselves that obsessive thoughts are **just thoughts**. They are not actual predictions of the future. Draw or describe any obsessive thoughts or images you have in these sandbags:

Imagine throwing the sandbags into the sea, never to bother you again.

If you decide you are committed to taking more control of your thoughts, what are some pleasurable topics you could choose to think about to replace negative or catastrophic thoughts?

Some examples are:

- Training to run a marathon
- My dream job
- A holiday
- How I celebrate my next birthday
- The last time I belly-laughed
- A person I feel close to
- A favourite hobby
- An enjoyable journey
- Spending an afternoon with friends

Either choose five topics of focus from these examples or make up your own. Use the following five pages to draw or paint images associated with these, or describe the details of where, how, who with, when...

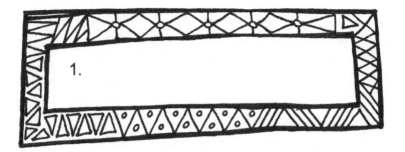

1.

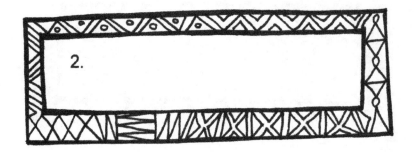

2.

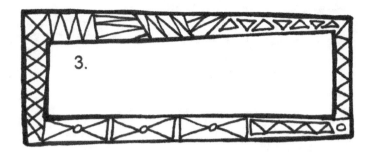

3.

4.

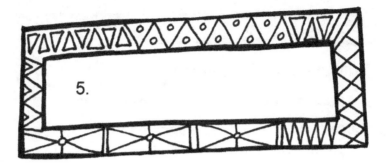

5.

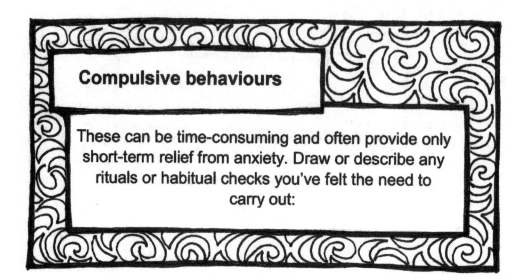

Compulsive behaviours

These can be time-consuming and often provide only short-term relief from anxiety. Draw or describe any rituals or habitual checks you've felt the need to carry out:

You may need to experiment with gradually reducing the number of times you carry these out, and use some of the techniques previously mentioned about 'sitting with' the feelings of anxiety, and addressing any negative or catastrophic thinking which often is the fuel behind compulsions.

Add up how much time you spend

doing these behaviours. In the last

week, this amounts to:

How else would you like to spend this time in the future? Remember that...

YOU CAN CHOOSE!!!

By experimenting with gradually reducing the number of times you act on compulsions, your confidence will increase that nothing catastrophic will happen by not carrying them out.

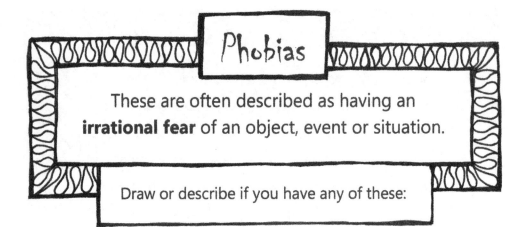

Phobias

These are often described as having an **irrational fear** of an object, event or situation.

Draw or describe if you have any of these:

The perception of danger can be quite low until we're presented with the trigger for our fear. Then unrealistic or catastrophic thinking usually increases very quickly.

If we're able to foresee any exposure to our feared object, event or situation, then using **relaxation techniques** beforehand can minimise anxiety.

Any sudden, unexpected exposure can be more challenging, and it's helpful to explore what thoughts are fuelling the fear.

Draw or describe some of the irrational thoughts you experience:

What would be some more realistic thoughts you could try and remember to say to yourself to **soothe** yourself and **challenge** the irrational thoughts?

For example...

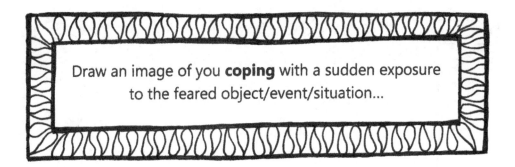

Draw an image of you **coping** with a sudden exposure to the feared object/event/situation...

PANIC

Colour in the symbols next to the statements

if you often:

Feel overwhelmed with intense fear

Experience light-headedness or dizziness

Find your heart racing or thumping

Experience difficulties breathing, e.g.

rapid, shallow breaths

or your throat feels constricted

Believe you're about to pass out

Experience an overwhelming urge to

escape from a situation

Believe others won't understand or help

if you start to feel panicky

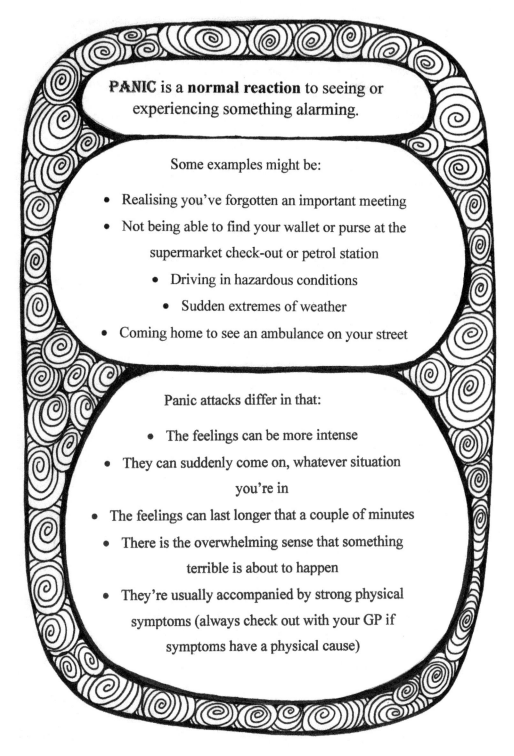

PANIC is a **normal reaction** to seeing or experiencing something alarming.

Some examples might be:

- Realising you've forgotten an important meeting
- Not being able to find your wallet or purse at the supermarket check-out or petrol station
- Driving in hazardous conditions
- Sudden extremes of weather
- Coming home to see an ambulance on your street

Panic attacks differ in that:

- The feelings can be more intense
- They can suddenly come on, whatever situation you're in
- The feelings can last longer that a couple of minutes
- There is the overwhelming sense that something terrible is about to happen
- They're usually accompanied by strong physical symptoms (always check out with your GP if symptoms have a physical cause)

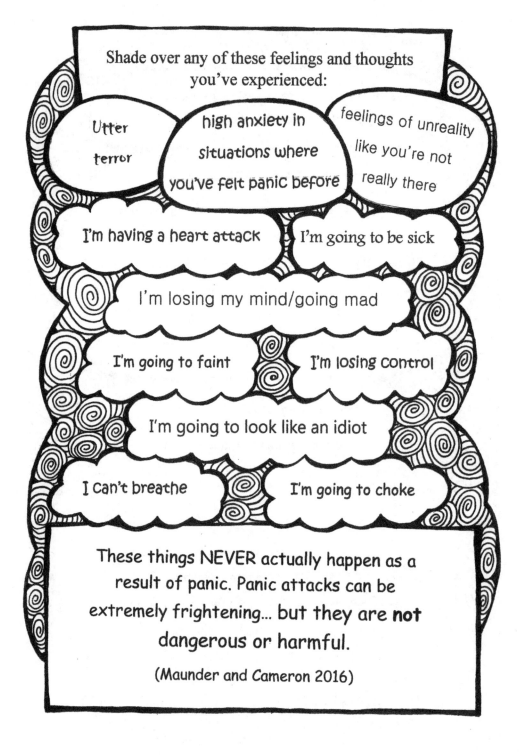

Shade over any of these feelings and thoughts you've experienced:

Utter terror

high anxiety in situations where you've felt panic before

feelings of unreality like you're not really there

I'm having a heart attack

I'm going to be sick

I'm losing my mind/going mad

I'm going to faint

I'm losing control

I'm going to look like an idiot

I can't breathe

I'm going to choke

These things NEVER actually happen as a result of panic. Panic attacks can be extremely frightening... but they are **not** dangerous or harmful.

(Maunder and Cameron 2016)

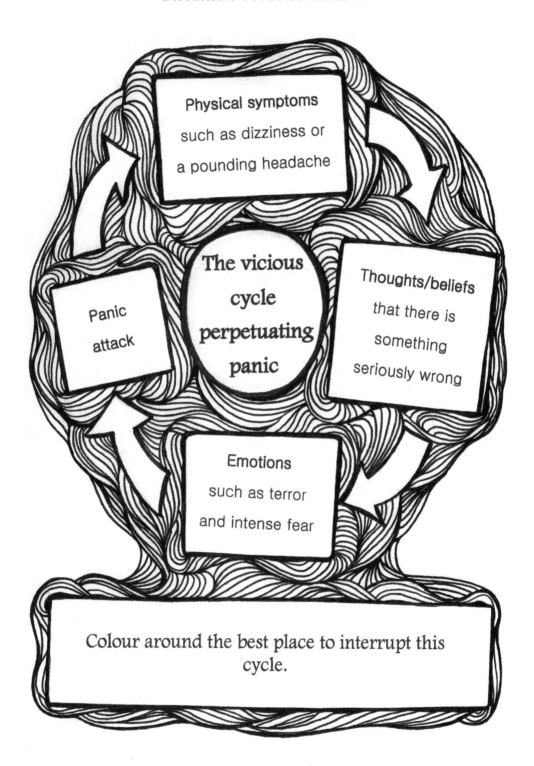

Physical symptoms such as dizziness or a pounding headache

The vicious cycle perpetuating panic

Panic attack

Thoughts/beliefs that there is something seriously wrong

Emotions such as terror and intense fear

Colour around the best place to interrupt this cycle.

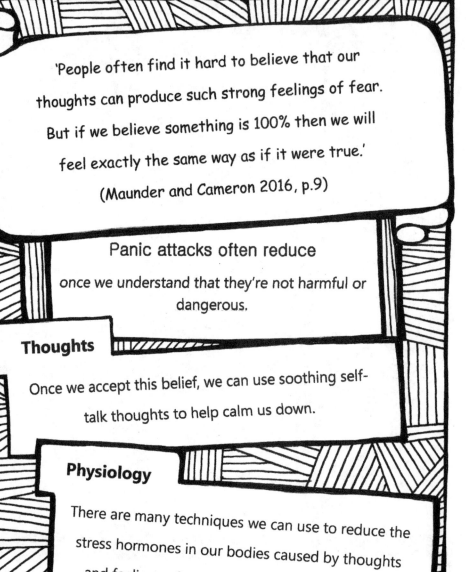

'People often find it hard to believe that our thoughts can produce such strong feelings of fear. But if we believe something is 100% then we will feel exactly the same way as if it were true.'
(Maunder and Cameron 2016, p.9)

Panic attacks often reduce once we understand that they're not harmful or dangerous.

Thoughts

Once we accept this belief, we can use soothing self-talk thoughts to help calm us down.

Physiology

There are many techniques we can use to reduce the stress hormones in our bodies caused by thoughts and feelings of panic. Most commonly used are relaxation techniques, mindful breathing techniques and exercising.

You've become an expert at using **calming** and **soothing** self-talk whenever you feel panic starting to rise. Draw an image of what this **calmness** looks and feels like.

When you've finished you could copy the colours you've used here to cover up the image on the previous page.

GENERAL ANXIETY

Colour in the symbols next to the statements,
if you often:

Find it difficult to relax

Believe something really awful is going to happen

Feel fidgety and restless

Spend loads of your time worrying

Find it difficult to concentrate whilst you're reading or watching TV

Find your sleep is affected:
It takes ages to fall asleep

Wake up several times during the night

Suddenly wake up feeling fearful

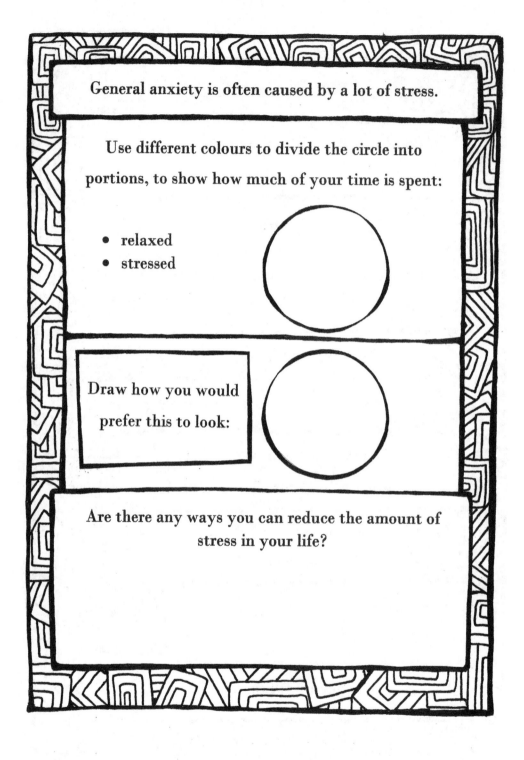

General anxiety is often caused by a lot of stress.

Use different colours to divide the circle into portions, to show how much of your time is spent:

- relaxed
- stressed

Draw how you would prefer this to look:

Are there any ways you can reduce the amount of stress in your life?

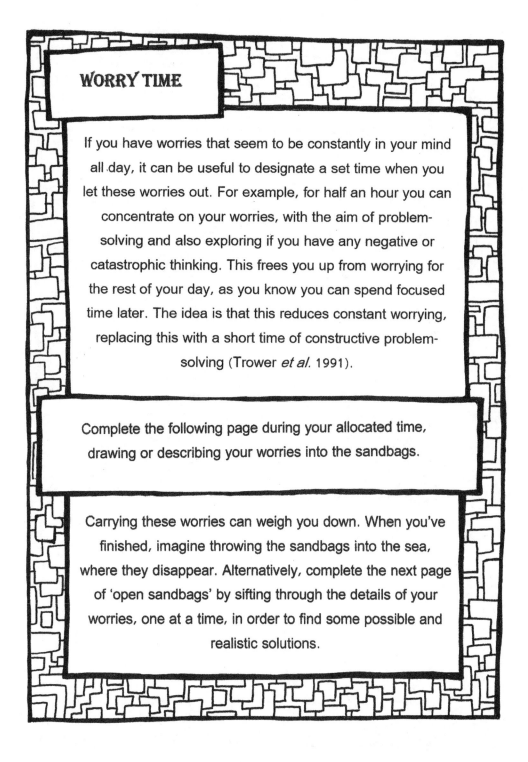

WORRY TIME

If you have worries that seem to be constantly in your mind all day, it can be useful to designate a set time when you let these worries out. For example, for half an hour you can concentrate on your worries, with the aim of problem-solving and also exploring if you have any negative or catastrophic thinking. This frees you up from worrying for the rest of your day, as you know you can spend focused time later. The idea is that this reduces constant worrying, replacing this with a short time of constructive problem-solving (Trower *et al.* 1991).

Complete the following page during your allocated time, drawing or describing your worries into the sandbags.

Carrying these worries can weigh you down. When you've finished, imagine throwing the sandbags into the sea, where they disappear. Alternatively, complete the next page of 'open sandbags' by sifting through the details of your worries, one at a time, in order to find some possible and realistic solutions.

Fill the sandbags with your worries…

Draw or describe some possible solutions...

9

Relaxation

Relaxation is...

- a skill

- something we inherently know how to do

- for lazy people

- essential for wellbeing

- a luxury I don't have time for

- something we do automatically

- for stressed, tense people

- boring

- important for good mental health

Colour in the symbols next to the statements you think are true.

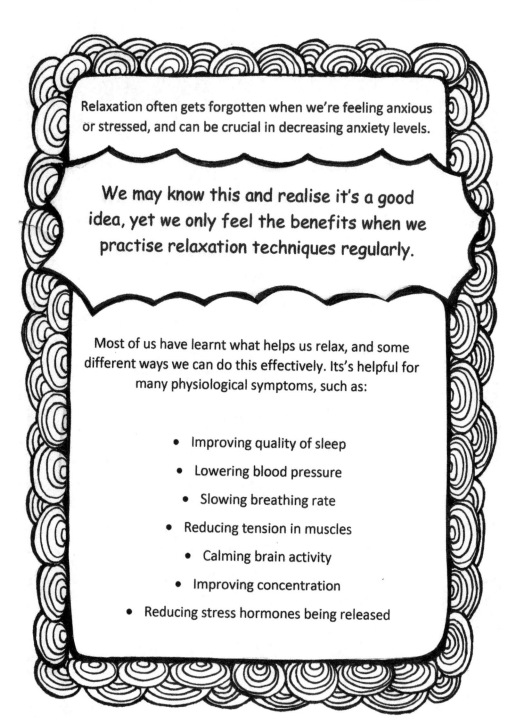

Relaxation often gets forgotten when we're feeling anxious or stressed, and can be crucial in decreasing anxiety levels.

We may know this and realise it's a good idea, yet we only feel the benefits when we practise relaxation techniques regularly.

Most of us have learnt what helps us relax, and some different ways we can do this effectively. Its's helpful for many physiological symptoms, such as:

- Improving quality of sleep
- Lowering blood pressure
- Slowing breathing rate
- Reducing tension in muscles
- Calming brain activity
- Improving concentration
- Reducing stress hormones being released

Definition:

A state of relaxation is when there is no anxiety or tension in the mind or body.

Draw or describe the last time you felt relaxed:

Only you can carve out some time in your daily life to devote to relaxation. It's more likely to happen if you decide now how regularly you'd like to give your time for doing this.

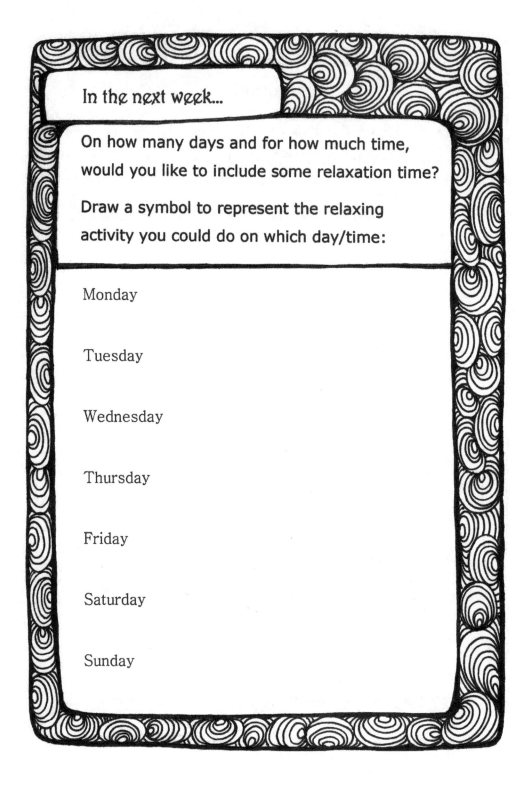

In the next week...

On how many days and for how much time, would you like to include some relaxation time?

Draw a symbol to represent the relaxing activity you could do on which day/time:

Monday

Tuesday

Wednesday

Thursday

Friday

Saturday

Sunday

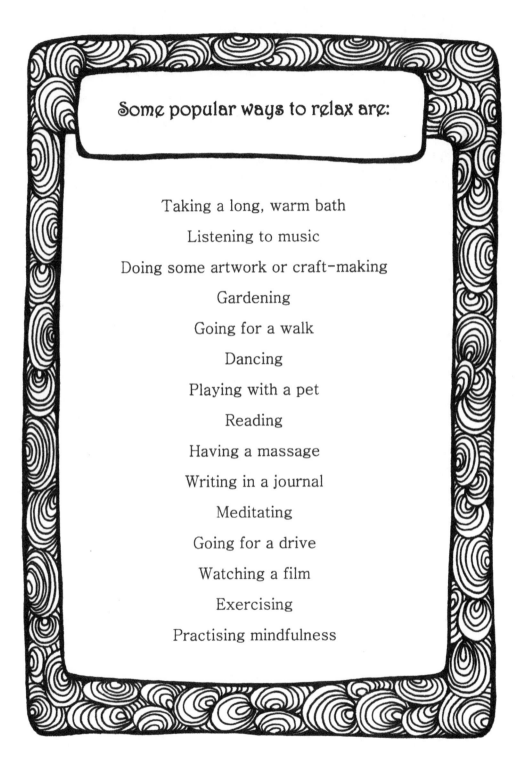

Some popular ways to relax are:

Taking a long, warm bath

Listening to music

Doing some artwork or craft-making

Gardening

Going for a walk

Dancing

Playing with a pet

Reading

Having a massage

Writing in a journal

Meditating

Going for a drive

Watching a film

Exercising

Practising mindfulness

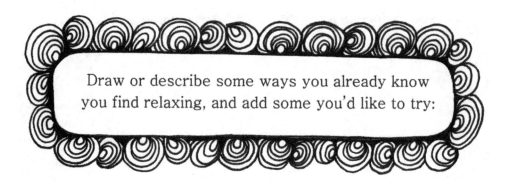

Draw or describe some ways you already know you find relaxing, and add some you'd like to try:

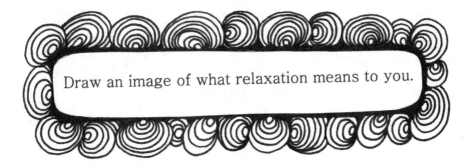

Draw an image of what relaxation means to you.

Mandalas

Mandalas are simply circular images, often created to elicit therapeutic change or to facilitate relaxation.

'While a mandala drawing will not magically reduce anxiety…studies have shown that drawing within a circular format can have calming physiological effects on the body in terms of heart rate and body temperature.' (Malchiodi 2007, p.127)

'For many people who are struggling with emotional problems, the mandala emerges spontaneously as a sign of change or transformation.'
(Malchiodi 2007, p.123)

Use the following four pages to create your own mandalas, with no other agenda than to see what emerges. Take notice also of how you feel before and after you've created the images, as there may be some differences between the images, depending on how anxious or relaxed you're feeling.

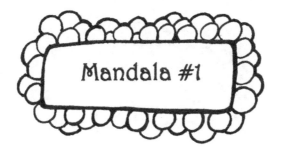

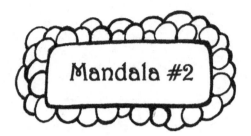

10

Taking Control

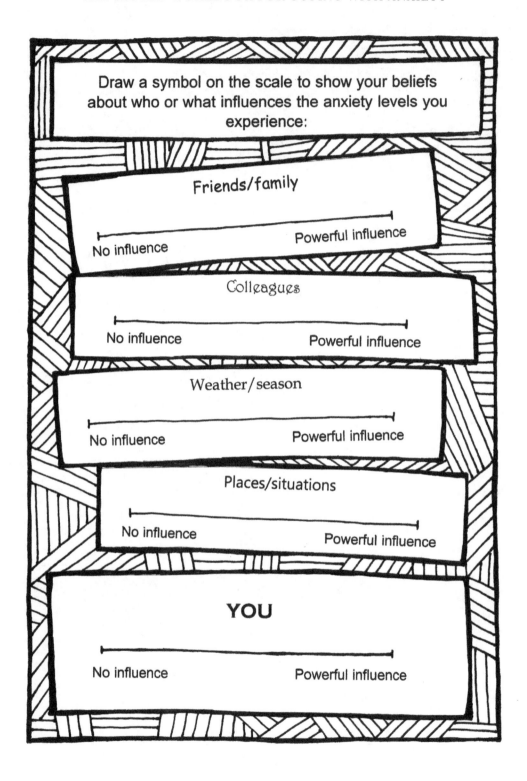

Draw a symbol on the scale to show your beliefs about who or what influences the anxiety levels you experience:

Friends/family

No influence — Powerful influence

Colleagues

No influence — Powerful influence

Weather/season

No influence — Powerful influence

Places/situations

No influence — Powerful influence

YOU

No influence — Powerful influence

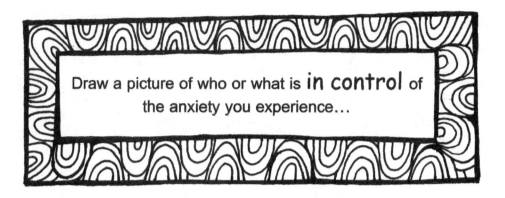

Draw a picture of who or what is **in control** of the anxiety you experience…

Imagine for a moment that your worst-case scenario happened. It's a few moments afterwards and you handled it WELL.

Draw an image here of what this would look and feel like...

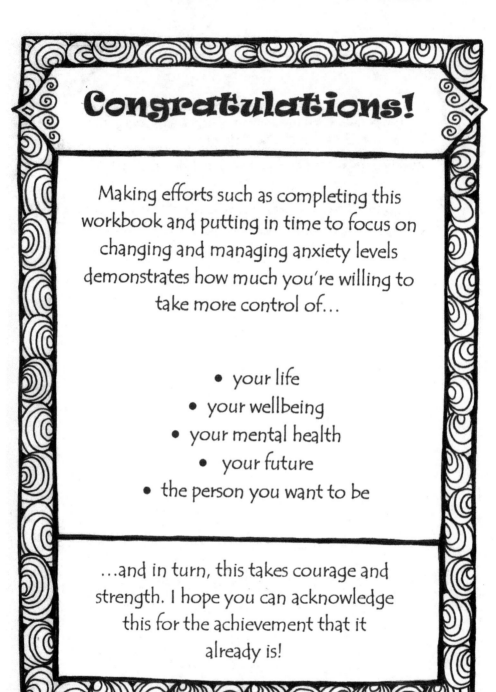

Congratulations!

Making efforts such as completing this workbook and putting in time to focus on changing and managing anxiety levels demonstrates how much you're willing to take more control of…

- your life
- your wellbeing
- your mental health
- your future
- the person you want to be

…and in turn, this takes courage and strength. I hope you can acknowledge this for the achievement that it already is!

References

Barford, D. (2018) 'Dark night of the soul.' *Therapy Today 29*, 6, 35.

Beck, J.S. (1995) *Cognitive Therapy: Basics and Beyond.* New York: Guildford Press.

Ellis, A. (1977) 'The Basic Clinical Theory of Rational Emotive Therapy.' In A. Ellis and R. Grainger (eds) *Handbook of Rational-Emotive Therapy.* New York: Springer.

Jenkins, P. (2017) *Professional Practice in Counselling and Psychotherapy.* London: Sage.

Kneeland, E.T., Dovidio, J.F., Joormann, J. and Clark, M.S. (2016) 'Emotion malleability beliefs, emotion regulation, and psychopathology: Integrating affective and clinical science.' *Clinical Psychology Review 45*, 81–88.

Layard, R. (2006) *The Depression Report: A New Deal for Depression and Anxiety Disorders.* London: Centre for Economic Performance, LSE. Accessed on 07/01/2019 at www.cep.lse.ac.uk/pubs/download/special/depressionreport.pdf.

London, P. (1989) *No More Secondhand Art: Awakening the Artist Within.* Boston, MA: Shambala.

Malchiodi, C.A. (2007) *The Art Therapy Sourcebook.* New York: McGraw Hill.

Manning, J. and Ridgeway, N. (2016) *CBT Worksheets for Anxiety.* Suffolk: West Suffolk CBT Service Ltd.

Maunder, L. and Cameron, L. (2016) *Anxiety and Panic.* Northumberland, Tyne and Wear NHS Foundation Trust.

McManus, S., Bebbington, P., Jenkins, R. and Brugha, T. (eds) (2016) 'Mental health and wellbeing in England: Adult psychiatric morbidity survey 2014.' Leeds: NHS digital on Mind.

Mercer, A., Warson, E. and Zhao, J. (2010) 'Visual journaling: An intervention to influence stress, anxiety and affect levels in medical students.' *The Arts in Psychotherapy 37*, 2, 143–148.

Neenan, M. and Dryden, W. (2004) *Cognitive Therapy: 100 Key Points and Techniques.* Hove: Brunner Routledge.

Trower, P., Casey, A. and Dryden, W. (1991) *Cognitive Behavioural Counselling in Action.* London: Sage.

Wilkinson, R. and Pickett, K. (2010) *The Spirit Level: Why Equality is Better for Everyone.* Harmondsworth: Penguin.

Winch, G. (2018) *Why You Should Believe You Can Control Your Emotions.* New York: Psychology Today. Accessed on 04/01/2019 www.psychologytoday.com/gb/blog/the-squeaky-wheel/201809/why-you-should-believe-you-can-control-your-emotions.

By the Same Author

The Art Activity Book for Psychotherapeutic Work
100 Illustrated CBT and Psychodynamic Handouts for Creative Therapeutic Work

Jennifer Guest

Paperback: £19.99 / $26.95
ISBN: 978 1 78592 301 2
eISBN: 978 1 78450 607 0

128 pages

Help clients to raise self-esteem, cope with change and adversity and manage complex emotions with these brand new 100 ready-to-use illustrated worksheets and activities.

Drawing on psychotherapeutic approaches including cognitive behavioural therapy (CBT), these worksheets are ideal for use in therapeutic work, for starting conversations and addressing problems that clients face. Each worksheet is designed to encourage clients to express their thoughts and emotions creatively in a relaxed way. The book also includes activities that centre on visual diary keeping, to help clients gain perspective on their unique issues and learn to solve their problems in a positive, healthy way.

Suitable for adults and young people, in individual or group work, this is an excellent resource for those who work in therapy, counselling and social work

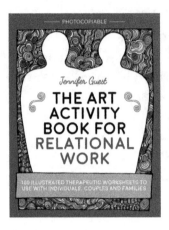

The Art Activity Book for Relational Work
100 illustrated therapeutic worksheets to use with individuals, couples and families

Jennifer Guest

Paperback: £17.99 / $29.95
ISBN: 978 1 78592 160 5
eISBN: 978 1 78450 428 1

128 pages

Explore and promote positive relationships with these 100 ready-to-use illustrated worksheets and activities.

Based on systemic theory, psychodynamic theory and cognitive behavioural therapy (CBT) principles, the activities are a creative approach to starting therapeutic conversations and engaging clients in their search for solutions. The photocopiable worksheets encourage clients to express their feelings through drawing, painting and writing. They are structured around four key areas: sense of self; partner relationships; family dynamics; and improving communication and conflict resolution. Activities include explanations of how and why they help to address specific relational issues.

Suitable for use by professionals working with individuals, couples or families in therapeutic situations, *The Art Activity Book for Relational Work* will help clients to resolve relational issues and strengthen bonds.

The CBT Art Activity Book
100 illustrated handouts for creative therapeutic work

Jennifer Guest

Paperback: £22.99 / $29.95
ISBN: 978 1 84905 665 6
eISBN: 978 1 78450 168 6

136 pages

Explore complex emotions and enhance self-awareness with these 100 ready-to-use creative activities.

The intricate, attractive designs are illustrated in the popular zentangle style and are suitable for adults and young people, in individual or group work. The worksheets use cognitive behavioural therapy (CBT) and art as therapy to address outcomes including improved self-esteem, emotional wellbeing, anger management, coping with change and loss, problem solving and future planning. The colouring pages are designed for relaxing stress management and feature a complete illustrated alphabet and series of striking mandala designs.